Playing with Fire
Hebrew Doorways to the Jewish Soul

Diane Rachel Bloomfield

AN ARTHUR KURZWEIL BOOK
New York/Jerusalem

Diane Rachel Bloomfield

Playing with Fire

Hebrew Doorways to the Jewish Soul

AN ARTHUR KURZWEIL BOOK

© 2024 by Diane Bloomfield
All rights reserved

No part of this book may be used or reproduced in any manner whatsoever without the prior express written permission of the author, except in the case of brief quotations embodied in critical articles and reviews. Please do not participate in or encourage piracy of copyrighted material in violation of the author's rights.

Edited by Wendy Bernstein

Cover and interior design by David Goldstein

Sages and Sources Section and Traditionally Scribed Hebrew Letters by Rabbi Dov Laimon

Back cover photogoraph by Sara H. Eichler

ISBN: 979-8-218-43269-0

I DEDICATE THIS BOOK
to my ancestors and all our children's children.
May the words of Torah be sweet in your mouths,
and teach you to know your name,
and God's goodness.

"Playing with Fire is simultaneously inviting and profound, accessible and aspirational. Bloomfield integrates classic Jewish texts into vignettes of her own life in ways that emerge as poetry for the heart and soul. Her love for Judaism and Israel becomes contagious for the reader. This book is a guide to all who seek out meaning and contemporary relevance in the study of Torah."

Rabbi Leon A. Morris
President, Pardes Institute of Jewish Studies, Jerusalem

"Diane's passionate journey of Torah learning guides us into a systematic approach for exploring Torah's hidden meaning. Her clearly articulated "Rules of Play" provide steps, examples and building blocks that readers can emulate to discover many facets of Biblical text. Her book beautifully demonstrates how Hebrew knowledge is critical in understanding deeper meanings of Torah."

Shirley Burdick
Founder and director of Ten Gentiles, a non-profit organization based in Jerusalem

"Diane Bloomfield's gift is in finding the essence of a teaching and bringing it to us with elegant simplicity and pristine clarity, so that our understanding becomes broader and deeper. Her use of Hebrew is masterful as she brings to life hidden gems of the Jewish sages. Whether we are beginners in the study of Judaism or seasoned scholars, Diane gives us a fresh framework to understand key concepts in Torah in ways that are richly layered, and profound."

Bracha Meshchaninov
Torah Educator and Yoga Therapist-Founder and Director of Tiferet Movement

"Diane Bloomfield offers a model of how to engage personally and meaningfully with Torah, interweaving her own story with the teachings that have illuminated her soul."

Ilana Kurshan
Author of If All the Seas Were Ink

"From the dynamic encounters between her personal explorations and journeys, and the depths of chassidic texts, Diane has gifted us with passion and candour with a creative book of teachings where Sfat Emet and other masters illuminate inner worlds and point to dimensions of ultimate meaning. Very grateful for this unique contribution."

Deena Garber
Teacher and researcher of chassidut and psychology in Jerusalem

Table of Contents

Acknowledgments *11*

How to Read and Study this Book *16*

1 *My Beginnings* *19*
- The Fiery Hebrew Letters
- The Sweet Taste of Sfat Emet
- First Dinner, then Dessert
- My Bobbie
- Sheina Punim and the Inner Point

2 *Playful Delight* *29*
- What is Torah?
- Our Books
- An Encounter with God's "Soul"
- Torah is a Gift
- God's Playful Delight
- God's Blueprint for Creation

3 *The Mystery of Hebrew* *39*
- What is Hebrew?
- God's First Creation
- God's Building Blocks
- God Dwells Inside the Letters
- God Spoke the World into Existence
- Sustaining the World with Hebrew Letters
- Letters and Words
- Sweet Starlight

4 Playing with Torah 50
- Torah Study Day and Night
- Transforming Study to Play
- Rules of Play
- Being a Student
- Deeply Rooted Renewal

5 Playing with B'reishit 61
- The First Letter
- The First Word
- Beginning with Torah
- Beginning with Israel
- Why Create with Torah and Israel?
- Continually Sustaining the World with Torah and Israel
- Torah is Hiding in All of Creation

6 Beginning with Sarah and Avraham 72
- Early Sightings
- Creating the World with Avraham
- Ancient Roots – Soul Mirrors
- Our Ancient Future Land
- Why Study Avraham and Sarah Now?
- One Secret Timeless Soul
- Sarah – The First Barren Mother
- The Root of עקרה Akara
- God's Role in the Birth of Yitzchak
- The Garden of the Matriarchs
- Revealing God to the World
- My Connection to Sarah
- "Nothing" was Her Child
- God Creates Yesh Me'ayin
- The Task of Returning Yesh to Ayin

7 Connecting to Holiness 95
- Mitzvahs are Connectors
- Candles and Light
- Torah Dressed as Action
- Food is Not Just Food
- Mitzvahs Add Life to Life
- Soul and Body
- Illuminating the Body of the World
- Weaving Garments of Light
- A Spiritual Scent
- Holiness
- Mitzvahs are Signposts to Holiness
- God is Hiding in the Word Mitzvah
- Separation for the Sake of Connecting
- Holiness and Chol

8 Heavenly Names - Secrets of the Yud 113
- Our Name and Our Soul
- Our Name and God's Name
- Clarifying Our Names Through Exile
- Exile as Boon
- Our Name is Our Book
- Sarai שרי – The Master of the Yud
- Harry Potter and the Hebrew Letters
- The Raw Material of all Letters
- The Transitional Point between the Infinite and the Finite
- Higher Wisdom and Yud
- One Dressed as Ten
- The Number Ten in Torah, Tradition, and the Human Body
- Deeper In: The Ten Sefirot

- The Hebrew Letters of ספירה Sefirah
- Sefirot: One of God's Garments
- Essence and Vessels
- The Ten Sefirot and the Body
- Ten that are One
- A Pictogram of the Sefirot
- Yud in Aleph – Doorway into Creation
- A Waterfall of Light
- Sarai Shares Her Yud
- He Will Laugh
- Laughter in the Land of Israel

9 *The Land that I Will Show You* *142*
- Children of the Future
- Field Trips to Holiness
- Jerusalem and B'reishit
- Glimpses of Our Razah D'Echad
- Sweet Sounds on the Train up to Jerusalem
- Piecing Together our Secret Oneness Puzzle
- Our Soul and the Hebrew Letters
- A New Reishit
- Laura and Mark's Story
- Our Names
- Rachel's Spiritual Watchtower
- My Connection to Rachel
- There is יש No End אין סוף

10 *Our Sages and Sources* *166*

Bibliography *193*

Acknowledgments

Writing a book is like climbing a mountain. At the beginning of your climb, you cannot see, or imagine, how you are going to get to the top. Often, you cannot even see the top. And then, of course, you realize what every experienced hiker knows: There is no way to foresee all the paths you are going to take, but you trust that the next step will always be right in front of you. And you can only climb one step at a time. Sometimes you feel like a rock climber on a precipitous slope, without a safety harness. At those moments you must bring absolute focus only to what is right in front of you in order to find a place for your hand or foot. When you settle into the present moment, you discover many treasures along the way.

From time to time, when you have your balance, it is helpful to look ahead to where you are going. Then one day, you take one more step, so focused in the present moment that you are surprised to discover you have arrived at the top. From there you have a good view of the many mountains that still lie ahead.

Whether you are hiking alone or with others, there are many helpers along the way. Sometimes help comes from a sturdy stone or solid tree branch. Sometimes it is the relief of a passing cloud that provides merciful shade, or the sun that warms up your cold bones. A comfortable resting place restores. A beautiful view inspires. A well-marked path reassures. Hiking partners lift you up the mountain on the wings of their good company.

I would like to thank all my wonderful and essential climbing companions who have helped me up the mountain of writing this book.

To my father, Coleman, whose memory brings so much blessing, and my mother, Shirley, may she continue to have good health and long life. Your enormously kind and generous hearts of love surround and support me, our whole family, and so many others. Your love and faith in me lift me up every mountain I climb.

And more thanks to you, Mom, for our home in Minnesota, where I spent so much time working on this book. For the many months each year that I spent with you, I wrote in a peaceful, solitary, quiet, spacious room with windows looking out over our tree-filled back yard, lush with emerald-green leaves, on fire with fall colors, sparkling with silent, magical, white snow. You turned the formidable writer's mountain into a comfortable, safe, loving home. The perfect writer's retreat. When I emerged from my mornings of writing, I loved reading you sections of my book, hot off the writing press. You were always eager to hear, and you are the world's greatest listener. Your feedback, and sometimes puzzled expressions, encouraged me and pushed me to write more clearly.

I also always love our precious time together, talking, walking, eating, playing games, and watching movies.

To my husband, Jonathan. Your enthusiasm and receptivity to the unexpected mystical ideas in this book, even though you are a self-proclaimed mitnaged (a non-mystical guy), delights me. Editing with you is such fun. Your slow, careful pace and patient attention to the smallest details of my writing adds beauty and clarity to the book. Your love and unmovable faith in me, my work, and this book, is the solid rock of the mountain of my life.

To my teacher, colleague, and friend, Rabbi Dov Laimon. Thanking you comes in story form:

Many years ago, I asked you to look at my book and give me feedback. After reading my manuscript, you said: "I think it would be good if we studied the sources together, to go deeper." And so we began to learn and work on the book together. You are a Torah scholar, teacher, scribe, and poet. Thank you for introducing me to a fabulously wide range of essential Torah sages and books and for writing the exquisite Sages and Sources chapter for this book. Everyone who reads it will be treated to the sweet and profound taste of the wisdom of our sages.

With kindness, you guided my writer's hand and heart with your subtle, scribally precise understandings. Walking together up this writing mountain we discovered and clarified treasures in every word and every thought of this book. Learning and writing with you is a delight for my soul.

There is more to this story. Dov and I were not the first ones in our families to walk together. After we met, we discovered that Dov's mom and my mom were friends when they were girls in Winnipeg, Manitoba, in the 1940s. They lived a few blocks from each other. My mom would knock on Dov's mom's door to walk with her to school. Like our moms, Dov and I live a block away from each other, but in Jerusalem, not Winnipeg. I too knock on his door to walk with him to school. I always try to imagine how utterly inconceivable it would have been to our mothers that their future children would live near each other in Jerusalem and work on a Torah book together. Our mothers were friends while World

War II and the Holocaust were raging in Europe in the 1940s and before Israel was a state. Dov and I also discovered that he was friends with my cousins on my dad's side in Saskatchewan, Canada. And then we found out that my great aunt Eta was married to his great uncle Jack. All these family connections, going back as far as a century, make our working together feel very *bashert* (Yiddish, destined to be).

To Arthur Kurzweil. You are always patiently waiting for me at the top of the mountain, smiling, loving, confident that I will make it. A few years ago, you encouraged me by saying: "You are writing this book for your children's children." That thought has fueled my writing and devotion to this book every step of the way.

To Wendy Bernstein. What a pleasure it is to work with you. I so appreciate your prompt, friendly, respectful, and orderly responses to all my questions. Your extensive editing knowledge is impressive and reassuring. Having you along is like taking an expert map reader on the hiking trail. There wasn't one edit you suggested that I didn't respond to with: "Of course! That clarifies the path."

To David Goldstein. For meeting me at the top of the mountain, patiently laying out the interior of the book with spacious clarity. And for designing beautiful, dancing, fiery Hebrew letters for the cover. You created an inviting, well marked path for the readers.

To my ancestors and the sages of the Jewish people and all my many, many Torah teachers. Thank you for blazing treasure-laden, illuminated trails for me to walk on as I find my way up the ancient, renewing mountain of Torah.

To my students. Your thirst for Torah and devotion to learning inspires me to climb higher and always seek more treasures.

To my family and friends. You are always my home in the world, even when we are far from each other. I am truly grateful for all your generous help and enthusiasm for my book. And to Laura and Mark: Thank you for making aliyah and providing me with the wonderful surprise ending for this book.

To all my dear nephews and nieces. So many of you love to hike; with this book I invite you to hike with me up the awesome mountain of Torah.

To my daughter, Kalya Tiferet. Like vibrant, colorful, spring wildflowers in Israel, your beauty and goodness fill my life with joy and *nachas* (Yiddish, spiritual pleasure). And thank you for bringing your Hebrew fluency to my Sfat Emet source citations.

Ultimately, of course, I thank God. King David's words are helpful here:

> **I lift up my eyes to the mountains, where will my help come from? My help is from God, the maker of heaven and earth** (Psalms 121:1).

Thank you, God, maker of heaven and earth, for creating the mountains I climb and abundantly providing all the help I need along the way.

How to Read and Study this Book

This book is an in-depth introduction to Torah through the wisdom of Jewish sages interwoven with my personal relationship to that wisdom.

I suggest reading this book in the order it is written, as I introduce many fundamental concepts and rules of play before I present in-depth teachings. There is a logical development to the teachings and stories I offer.

You can also open this book at any page and dive in. After all, the great work of rabbinic thought, the Talmud, begins on page ב (*bet*), the second letter of the Hebrew alphabet, rather than page א (*aleph*), the first letter. This hints that we are always stepping into the middle of an ongoing story when we study Torah.

When you study the Torah teachings, slow down your pace. Read the teachings more than once. Mull them over. Close your eyes and contemplate their wisdom. Study with a partner. Studying Torah is different than most reading. Although I have endeavored to clarify the teachings, it still takes time to understand Torah and our profound sages. As the Rabbis say:

> **The one who studies Torah 100 times cannot be compared to the one who studies it 101 times** (Babylonian Talmud, Chagiga 9:b).

Each time we go over a Torah teaching, it reveals more, and our understanding grows.

Sarah and Avraham, the first mother and father of the Jewish people, play an essential part in this book. When they first appear in the Torah, they are called Sarai and Avram. Later, God changes their names to Sarah and Avraham. I use their original names when I offer a teaching about those names or when I quote from the Torah.

MY PERSONAL STORIES BEGIN WITH the first five words in capitals.

Indented bold paragraphs are quotes. Direct quotes from English texts have quotation marks around them. All other indented bold paragraphs are my translations.

The fiery Hebrew word on the cover is שעשעי *(shaashuai)* my delight. It is found in the verse:

> **If your Torah were not my delight I would be lost in my distress** (Psalms 119:92).

Torah is God's delight. Torah is my delight.

My hope is that the spacious design layout of this book offers breathing room and open spaces for you to discover the delight of living Torah in your life.

1
My Beginnings

The Fiery Hebrew Letters

WHEN I WAS A LITTLE girl, I fell in love with Hebrew. The letters looked like fire to me. Before I could even read, my whole being was drawn into the mysterious beauty of the Hebrew letters in the prayer book. Their fiery shapes delighted my soul with whispered promises of stories, secrets, and meaning.

The first time I remember being jealous was the day my older brother, Leon, started Hebrew school. I could hardly wait until the following year when it would be my turn to start learning to read the mysterious letters that danced in my heart and burned in my soul. I couldn't believe that someone could teach me to read those fiery shapes.

When my first day of class finally arrived, there was no place in the whole world I wanted to be more than in my seat in Hebrew school. That plain undecorated room, that simple blackboard, that piece of chalk, and that elderly lady, Mrs. Apt, were the keys to a world that my soul already knew was my true home. Nothing could have been more true than my response to the attendance call: אני פה *(ani po)* I am here! I was eagerly present, bouncing with joy, and totally attentive when Mrs. Apt wrote the א (*aleph*) up on the board and taught me its name. Thank you, Mrs. Apt!

As I see it now, my whole life has been a continuation of that first moment in Hebrew school. I am still in Mrs. Apt's simple classroom, transfixed by the aleph on the board and the aleph in my heart. I am still longing to discover the mystery of its flames. The more I look, the deeper my longing grows to stay very close to these soul-enlivening secrets.

My love of Hebrew eventually led me to the study of Torah. As a child, I had seen the fire in the Hebrew letters. As an adult, I learned that Torah is called fire.

> **God says: My word is fire** (Jeremiah 23:29).

In the Zohar we find:

> **The Torah that God gave Moses is black fire written on white fire** (Zohar 3:132a).

The black fire is the wisdom of the written letters and words of the Torah. The white fire is the expansive spaces between and behind the letters, the Torah's wordless wisdom. For more than forty years, I have been blessed to live in Jerusalem, learning with profound teachers, immersed in the study of this fire.

In this book I offer tastes from my studies and experiences of the fire of Torah, organized into a systematic Hebrew-based approach to Torah study.

The Sweet Taste of Sfat Emet

At the heart of my studies lie the teachings of Rabbi Yehudah Aryeh Leib Alter, whom I first "met" more than thirty years ago.

Rabbi Yehudah Aryeh Leib Alter, the Sfat Emet, was the third Rebbe of the Ger chassidic dynasty in the late 1800s in Poland. The Ger chassidim were the largest and most influential chassidic group in Poland before the Holocaust. They are still one of the largest chassidic groups, many of them living in Israel.

The first Ger Rebbe was Sfat Emet's beloved grandfather and teacher, Rabbi Isaac Meir Rothenberg, the Chidushei HaRim. During his lifetime, the Chidushei HaRim suffered the loss of many of his sixteen children. After a life-threatening illness, his beloved son, Abraham Mordechai, miraculously fathered one son, Yehudah Leib. Abraham Mordechai died when Yehudah Leib was eight. The Chidushei HaRim poured his heart and soul into teaching his precious grandson. Yehudah Leib lived, day and night, in the great light of his grandfather's profound faith and teachings.

When Yehudah Leib got married, his grandfather instructed him to change his name to Yehudah Aryeh Leib, so that he would not have the same name as his father-in-law.

When the Sfat Emet was nineteen, his grandfather died. Recognizing his greatness, the community wanted the Sfat Emet to become the next Rebbe of Ger, but he refused. Rabbi Chanoch Henikh HaKohen Levin, a disciple of the Chidushei HaRim, took the position. When he died four years later, the Sfat Emet very reluctantly accepted the position as the third Rebbe of Ger.

Sfat Emet led his community for thirty-five years until his death in 1905. Each Shabbat he taught his unique insights on the Torah. After Shabbat he wrote them up in Hebrew. Tens of thousands of chassidim would come from near and far to be in the presence of their beloved Rebbe, to learn from him, and to get his advice on every aspect of their lives. His teachings were compiled into books by his children.

The concluding sentence of his last teaching was:

> שפת אמת תכון לעד *(Sfat emet tikon l'ad)* **The language of truth will last forever** (Proverbs 12:19).

His children called the entire collection of their father's teachings Sfat Emet: The Language of Truth.

> **The son of the Sfat Emet, Rabbi Abraham Mordechai Alter, the Imrei Emet, said his father wanted every Jew to be able to understand his Torah teachings** (Shlomo Rosenberg, Tikon L'Ad, page 8).

And to this day, the Sfat Emet's teachings are studied widely throughout the Jewish world.

First Dinner, then Dessert

MY SOUL HAS ALWAYS BEEN drawn to chassidic and kabbalistic teachings that present the more secret, mystical levels of Torah. Even so, I knew that studying the mystical teachings without a solid grounding in traditional texts would be like eating a very sweet dessert before dinner. I felt it would lead to spiritual indigestion. So I nourished myself at the Pardes Institute of Jewish Studies in

Jerusalem with the bread-and-butter traditional texts of Jewish learning, like the Bible and the Talmud. The sages of the mystical teachings of Torah were all deeply rooted in the study of these texts. After spending five years at the solid breakfast, lunch, and dinner of Torah learning at Pardes, my soul was ready for dessert. I was thirsty and hungry for the sweet tastes of the hidden levels of Torah study.

After my years at Pardes I moved to Boston for a few years where I continued to study Torah. I was introduced to Sfat Emet's Chanukah teachings in a class given by a lay member of the Boston Jewish community, Janet Zimmerman. My love of Sfat Emet, like my love of Hebrew, was instantaneous. How can I describe the delight I experienced in this first encounter? Sfat Emet's wisdom went straight into my heart and soul, giving voice to the Hebrew letters that had been burning inside me since I was a child. From that moment on, Sfat Emet has been my constant spiritual companion. I study his teachings almost every day. In his words, I hear the voice of my soul.

How perfect that Sfat Emet's illuminating words first reached me on Chanukah, a holiday that celebrates miraculous light. Thank you, Janet Zimmerman, for lighting the first Sfat Emet candle for me.

Teachers never know what they are offering their students. Little did I foresee that I would spend my life diving always deeper into Sfat Emet's endlessly renewing thought. Little did I dream that I would become a teacher of his wisdom.

My Bobbie

IN THAT FIRST SFAT EMET class in Boston, I encountered the concept of הנקודה הפנימית *(hanekudah hapnimit)* the inner point. I will introduce the inner point with a story about my Bobbie.

Bobbie was what we called my mother's mother. Bobbie is an American pronunciation of the Yiddish word for grandmother, Bubbie. Like Sfat Emet, my Bobbie came from Poland. When she was a little girl in the shtetl (Yiddish, small town) of Rosvadorf, Sfat Emet was the Rebbe in Ger, a distance of only 125 miles from her town. For sure the Jews of her town, and maybe even Bobbie herself, knew of Sfat Emet and heard some of his teachings. It is even possible that my Bobbie's father, my great-grandfather Menachem, who was a learned man, traveled to Ger to hear the Sfat Emet teach.

The Aramaic expression מה דלבה לפומא לא גליא *(mah d'libah l'fuma la galya)* the mouth cannot reveal what is in the heart touches on the impossible task of finding words for expressing the love in my heart for my Bobbie. She was made entirely of love. She was the warmest, kindest, gentlest person I knew. And this is saying a lot, as I was raised in a large family of warm, kind, and very gentle people.

Just as for Sfat Emet, Yiddish was my Bobbie's first language. She had that wonderful old-world Yiddish accent when she spoke English. My Bobbie and my mother often spoke Yiddish with each other. When Bobbie would visit from Winnipeg, we would pick her up from the train station. On those car rides home, she and my mother would catch up with each other, talking in Yiddish. Although I didn't understand Yiddish, I loved hearing them talk. In their incomprehensible conversations, I heard so much love.

I felt so much heart. It was the love between my mother and her mother. It was the heart of a tradition, my tradition, calling out to me, beating inside of me.

Bobbie was my link to a world that was almost entirely lost, the world of the Jews of Eastern Europe. From her Yiddish accent and loving ways I knew that I was Jewish. I recognized that I was connected to a people I needed and wanted to be part of. I realized that I was an essential link in a tradition I needed and wanted to pass on to my own children.

Beginning with the first Jewish parents, Sarah and Avraham, Jewish parents have always passed on Judaism, from one generation to the next, with urgent devotion and profound love. Much like Sfat Emet, who received his Judaism from his grandfather's heart-filled Torah teachings, I received my Judaism from my grandmother's heart-filled Jewish essence. As a child I used to worry about how my children would know they were Jewish if they never heard Yiddish. How would they know they were Jewish if they didn't know Bobbie?

Sheina Punim and the Inner Point

WHEN I WAS A LITTLE girl, my parents used to ask me: "What does sheina punim mean?" I would answer: "It means Bobbie is coming." Of course, the Yiddish saying sheina punim does not mean Bobbie is coming — it means beautiful face. But because that is what my Bobbie would say when she would see me and my siblings, for me it meant Bobbie is coming.

Let's look deeper into sheina punim. Punim is the Yiddish pronunciation of the Hebrew word פנים *(panim)* face. The letters of panim are also in the word בפנים *(bifnim)* inside. They are also in the word פנימיות *(pnimiyut)* inwardness. Hebrew reveals that there is a connection between our outer face and what is inside of us, our inner face.

In English the word face is singular. In Hebrew the word פנים *(panim)* face is plural. If we were to translate the word panim literally, we would have to say faces. This seems to be closer to reality. Every person has many faces. In fact, all of reality has many faces. But inside all the outer faces of reality there is one inner face. That one inner face is the essential, life-giving, divine source of all the outer faces. That divine inner face is what Sfat Emet calls הנקודה הפנימית *(hanekudah hapnimit)* the inner point or simply הנקודה *(hanekudah)* the point. This one inner face is the sheina punim, the beautiful, divine inner face of the world.

Sfat Emet teaches us to look within all the outer faces of reality for the one beautiful face of God. Discovering this point inside everything is the essential purpose of creation. He calls this spiritual turning toward the inner point פנימיות *(pnimiyut)* inwardness. The Jewish people, with God's help, have faithfully passed on knowledge of the inner point from generation to generation.

> **God guards this inner point so that it will remain within the Children of Israel** (Sfat Emet, Chanukah תרל״א ד״ה זאת חנוכה).

The inner point is the central theme of Sfat Emet's teachings; it is the heartbeat of his thought.

THANK YOU, BOBBIE, FOR PASSING on to me the great gift of being Jewish and showing me the sheina punim of the world. I felt it beating in your kind heart when we hugged. I saw it peering out from your loving eyes. I heard it in your voice, in your Yiddish conversations with my mother, and in your fast and fluent reading of the Hebrew words at our Passover seders. I tasted it in your cinnamon buns, which we called Bobbie buns. I witnessed it in the quiet, humble dignity with which you ate only kosher food.

Sfat Emet received Torah from his grandfather. His great desire was to pass it on to those after him. I received my love of Judaism from my grandmother, my Bobbie. I also want to pass my love of Torah on to others.

To begin with, we must consider what Torah is.

2

Playful Delight

What Is Torah?

If someone asked you, "What is Torah?" what would you say? There are as many ways to answer this question as there are people to ask. Actually, there are more answers than there are people to ask, as many people have multiple answers. Here are a few:

To begin with, the Hebrew word תורה *(Torah)* literally means teaching. According to Rabbi Yehudah Loew ben Bezalel, the Maharal of Prague:

> **Torah is called teaching because it teaches a person the way to reach his ultimate purpose** (Netiv HaTorah, Netivot Olam, Chapter 1).

Our Books

Torah comprises many books. Here is an introduction to a few of the essential ones.

Torah is Chumash, which comes from the word חמש *(chamesh)* five. Chumash is the Five Books of Moses, known in English as Genesis, Exodus, Leviticus, Numbers, and Deuteronomy, which tell the stories of the creation of the world; of the patriarchs, matriarchs, and birth of the Jewish people; of the exile and redemption of the

Jews from Egypt; of their receiving the Torah; and of their forty years in the desert, preparing to enter the Land of Israel.

Torah is Nevi'im, Prophets, which tell the stories of the prophets, judges, and kings of Israel, beginning with Joshua entering the Land of Israel and including Samuel, Isaiah, Jeremiah, Ezekiel, up to the time of Malachi, the last prophet, at the beginning of the Second Temple period.

Torah is K'tuvim, Writings, works of faith, poetry, prayer, story, and wisdom, including Psalms, Proverbs, Job, Song of Songs, Ruth, Esther, and several more.

Torah is the compilation of the **T**orah (five books of Chumash), **N**evi'im (Prophets), and **K**'tuvim (Writings), called by the acronym תנ״ך *(Tanach)*. The letter כ *(kaf)* is pronounced K at a beginning of a word and Ch at the end of a word. The Tanach is also called the Written Torah.

Torah is Midrash, the multiple volumes of rabbinic literature that expand and illuminate the Tanach. Midrash includes Midrash Rabbah, Tanchuma, Mechilta, Sifra, Sifrei, and more.

Torah is Talmud, a compilation of Mishnah and Gemara, works of razor-sharp law, passionate arguments, and real and imagined legends. The enormous sea of Talmud and Midrash is also called the Oral Torah.

Torah is Kabbalah, primarily based on the teachings of the Zohar, The Book of Radiance, which illuminates the hidden and ever-revealing story of God's relationship to the Jewish people and all of creation. According to the Zohar, the stories and laws in Torah are the outer garment and body of the inner spiritual essence of Torah.

Torah is books of Jewish law such as the Shulchan Aruch by Rabbi Yosef Caro and the Mishneh Torah by Maimonides — codifications of the laws discussed in the Talmud.

Torah is Chassidut, the thoughts and teachings that began with Rabbi Israel ben Eliezer, the Baal Shem Tov, in eighteenth-century Ukraine. Chassidic Torah longs to draw the light and meaning of Torah into the heart and mind of every Jew.

Torah is commentaries to all Torah mentioned above by countless sages spanning thousands of years, including Rashi, Yehudah HaLevi, Rambam, Ramban, Maharal, Vilna Gaon, Sfat Emet, Abraham Isaac Kook, Abraham Joshua Heschel, Nechama Leibowitz, and Adin Steinsaltz.

Torah is also the ongoing story of the Jewish people that is still being written. My story, your story, the story of our children and beyond, are ever-expanding chapters of Torah.

An Encounter with God's "Soul"

Even if we knew all the books in the Jewish library, we still would not have a complete answer to the question, "What is Torah?" Another dimension to Torah is hidden in the word אנכי *(anochi)*, the first word of the Ten Commandments. Simply translated, אנכי *(anochi)* means I. But Rabbi Yochanan in the Talmud reads אנכי *(anochi)* as a four-letter acronym that reveals that God has written His Soul into the Torah.

    אנא *(ana)* I
    נפשי *(nafshi)* my Soul
    כתבת *(katavit)* have written
    יהבת *(yehevit)* have given

> **I have written and given my Soul** (Babylonian Talmud, Shabbat 105a).

When God reveals the Torah to the Children of Israel, He whispers a great secret in the letters of אנכי *(anochi)*. Torah is not an ordinary book. Torah is the Soul of God.

We can never fully know even what our own soul is, let alone the Soul of God. When we say "the Soul of God," we must know the basic Torah principle that:

> **Torah talks in the language of man** (Babylonian Talmud, Brachot 31b).

When Torah describes God with images from our world, like the eye of God, the hand of God, God's anger, God's joy, it uses human language — not as a literal description of God, but as a poetic hint to the spiritual, as metaphor for a higher reality.

Because God gave His Soul in the Torah,

> **Torah is** an encounter with the Soul of God.

Just as we can never fully know God, we can never fully know Torah.

Torah is a Gift

Moses was the greatest of the prophets and the ultimate Torah teacher. He had private Torah lessons with God on Mount Sinai for forty days and forty nights. But, according to the Midrash, even Moses had a hard time understanding Torah.

> Rabbi Abahu said that, for all of the forty days that Moses was up on the mountain with God, he was learning Torah — and then forgetting it! In the end he said to God, "Master of the world, it has been forty days and I don't know anything." What did the Holy One do? After he completed the forty days, **He gave him the Torah as a gift** (Midrash Tanchuma, Ki Tisa 16).

Sfat Emet explains:

> After all his efforts for forty days, Moses was not able to receive Torah until it was given to him as a gift. It is through great effort that we merit the gift of Torah, which is not possible by mere human comprehension. Rather, the Holy One gives Torah as a gift, according to the extent of the **efforts of the person** (Sfat Emet, Ki Tisa תרנ"ד ד"ה בפסוק).

Even Moses could not understand Torah without the help of God. Great effort is necessary, but not sufficient, for comprehending Torah. After God saw that Moses put in great effort, He gave him the whole Torah as a gift.

WE TOO HAVE THE POTENTIAL to receive the gift of Torah. It is in our hands to knock on heaven's door with our efforts. It is in God's hands to open the door and give us Torah. In my Torah study, I often experience this process of knocking on heaven's door with my efforts to comprehend, hoping the door will open and I will receive the gift of Torah. How many nights have I fallen into bed exhausted, my head spinning with lack of understanding of a particular idea I am studying! And then, when I wake up, I have clearer comprehension. The experience is that of receiving a gift — a gift greater than I could have imagined.

God's Playful Delight

One of my favorite answers to "What is Torah?" is, perhaps, surprising.

Torah is God's playful delight.

This is most likely not the first answer that comes to mind. But playful delight is one of the oldest descriptions of Torah. In the book of Proverbs, we discover that Torah was God's playful delight even before creation. Speaking in the first person, Wisdom tells her own story. The Rabbis understand that Wisdom and Torah are one.

> "The Lord created me at the beginning of His course, As the first of His works of old. In the distant past I was fashioned, At the beginning, at the origin of earth. There was still no deep when I was brought forth, No springs rich in water; Before [the foundation of] the mountains were sunk, Before the hills, I was born. He had not yet made earth and fields, Or the world's first clumps of clay. I was there when He set the heavens into place; When He fixed the horizon upon the deep; When He made the heavens above firm, And the fountains of the deep gushed forth; When He assigned the sea its limits, So that its waters never transgress His command, When He fixed the foundations of the earth" (Proverbs 8:22-29 *The Jewish Publication Society Hebrew-English Tanakh*).

After describing how she was with God before creation, Wisdom/Torah describes her relationship with God:

> I was with Him as an אמון *(amon)* confidant, a daily delight, playing before Him in every moment (Proverbs 8:30).

Similar to the fiery Hebrew letters that danced in delightful play before me as a child, the fire of Torah danced in delightful play before God, even before the world was created.

Calling Torah God's playful delight does not trivialize Torah. It raises it higher, fulfilling one of its most lofty purposes — bringing delight to the world.

As King David said, more than three thousand years ago:

> **If your Torah were not my delight, I would be lost in my distress** (Psalms 119:92).

God's Blueprint for Creation

We find more answers to "What is Torah?" in the word אמון *(amon)* from the verse in Proverbs. As we saw above, one translation of אמון *(amon)* is confidant, but there are lots of other meanings. What are they? Sounds like a simple question, right? Ha! Suffice it to say that my attempts to understand this word and translate this verse clearly have stymied me time after time. Throughout my twelve years of working on this book, I have returned over and over again to this verse.

IN ONE OF MY MANY attempts to understand the word אמון *(amon)* I turned to my teacher, colleague, and friend Rabbi Dov Laimon. One day, as we were poring over the microscopically small-worded, extensive commentaries struggling to clarify the multilevel understandings of this word, I looked pleadingly to Dov for help. We just laughed and continued to learn. I have realized that it is precisely these kinds of humbling encounters with the study of Torah that I want to portray in this book. Because Torah is a divine gift we receive after putting in great effort, I invite you to join me in knocking on heaven's door in my efforts to understand the word אמון *(amon)*.

Midrash Rabbah offers five different meanings for amon:

> **The great Rabbi Hoshaya said: I was an אמון *(amon)* to Him, a source of daily delight, playing before him at all times. Amon means learning. Amon means covered. Amon means hidden. And there is one who says amon means great… Alternatively, amon means אמן *(uman)* artisan's tool** (Midrash Rabbah, B'reishit 1:1).

Rabbi Mordechai Yosef Leiner of Isbitza, the Mei HaShiloach, teaches that each of these five meanings of amon represents one stage in the development of Torah, from its concealed beginnings in the mind of God to its full revelation as God's tool in creating the world.

The development of Torah is like the stages in the development of a human being. In the first stage, the human being is utterly hidden; this is the concealed moment of conception. In the second stage, the fetus is covered, growing in its mother's womb, preparing for birth. In the third stage, the baby has been born and is nursing; it is dependent on the mother yet beginning to recognize its environment (learning). The fourth stage is maturity (greatness); the child has been weaned and is more active and independent in its own life. The fifth stage is when the child, grown to adulthood, becomes a parent and brings forth the next generation; this is the stage of becoming God's partner in creation (the artisan's tool).

> **So too with Torah — its beginnings are utterly hidden in the essence of God. Torah develops covered, imperceptible to the world it is destined to enter. Next, Torah emerges out of its hidden place, yet is still totally bound to and nurtured by its source (learning). Then, Torah develops to maturity**

> (greatness). Finally, Torah becomes God's tool for creating the world (Mei HaShiloach, B'reishit, aleph).

The Midrash elaborates:

> I was the artisan's tool of the Holy One. In the way of the world, a king of flesh and blood who builds a castle does not do so from his own knowledge, but rather from the knowledge of an אמן *(uman)* artisan, and the artisan also does not build it from his own knowledge, but rather he has scrolls and books, (a blueprint) in order to know where to make rooms and doors. So too the Holy One looked into the Torah and created the world (Midrash Rabbah, B'reishit 1:1).

The blueprint is the artisan's tool. The Torah is the deep structure of the world. Everything in creation is an aspect of Torah. Looking deeply into creation, we can discover Torah everywhere. Just as my whole life is a journey revealing the secrets of my soul, all of creation is a journey revealing the delightful secrets of Torah hidden in the world.

No single answer, however deep and comprehensive, can fully define what Torah is. When I asked my mother "What is Torah?" she said, "I don't know. After all your lessons, I still don't know." I took this as a compliment that I had, at the very least, presented something of the mystery of Torah in my teachings.

This book is an invitation to the delightful, playful study of Torah. To prepare for study, it is helpful to know a few things about Hebrew and the tradition of Torah study.

3
The Mystery of Hebrew

What Is Hebrew?

To begin, I would like to proclaim and explain my passionate conviction that Hebrew is one of the most powerful keys to Torah secrets. When studying Torah in Hebrew, every story, every word, every letter, is a doorway into spiritual worlds. Knowing a few things about Hebrew clarifies why it is so powerful.

There are many ways to describe what Hebrew is. One can present Hebrew from a linguistic perspective, focusing on grammar and syntax. One can present Hebrew from an academic perspective, focusing on the history and development of the language. I am drawn mostly to the mystical, spiritual elements of Hebrew. In this book, I will present Hebrew from that perspective.

After many unsuccessful attempts to write about Hebrew, I turned again to Dov Laimon for help. As well as being a dedicated student and profound teacher of Torah for more than forty years, Dov is a Torah scribe. He spends his days in profound concentration, writing Hebrew letters with quill and ink onto parchment, creating sacred Jewish texts. He has also been teaching the wisdom of the Hebrew letters for decades. And yet, when Dov and I tried to articulate a clear description of Hebrew and Hebrew letters, we were silent for quite a while.

It is comforting to know that Dov and I are in good company. The study of the spiritual depth of Hebrew has occupied the greatest of the Jewish mystics and scholars throughout the centuries.

> **There is no measuring or evaluating the secrets and mysteries that are hidden in even one letter of the Torah** (Sfat Emet, B'shalach תרל"א ד"ה אז ישיר).

> **There is no end or complete understanding of the twenty-two letters of the Torah.... They are endlessly expanding. The essence of the inner secrets of the letters has no end** (Sfat Emet, B'shalach תרס"ד ד"ה אז ישיר).

According to Rabbi Moshe Cordovero, the Ramak, there are four levels of Torah. The first level is the stories of the Torah. The second level is the commandments. The third level is the Kabbalah. The fourth level is the Hebrew letters.

These levels are compared to the clothing, the body, the soul, and the soul of the soul. The Hebrew letters are the most hidden realm. Understanding their depth is extremely rare. At this level we are approaching the Hidden Soul that enlivens everything.

> **The fourth level is the spirituality of the letters, their connections and relationships with each other. The one who goes down into the depth of this matter can create worlds. This level is called the soul of the soul** (Pardes Rimonim, Gateway of the Letters, Chapter 1).

We see that Hebrew is infinitely more than a language developed by people for the sake of ordinary communication. Hebrew letters are more than two-dimensional shapes on a page representing speech. They are the endlessly expanding soul of the soul of the world.

God's First Creation

In most languages, writing and reading are created after speaking. Writing and reading are a representation of speech. With Hebrew, however, the letters preceded the spoken word. Actually, the Hebrew letters preceded everything in the created world. They were one of God's first creations. This is hinted at in the beginning of the Torah.

> בראשית *(B'reishit)* In the beginning
> ברא אלקים *(bara Elokim)* God created
> את *(et)*
> השמים *(hashamayim)* the heavens (B'reishit 1:1).

Grammatically, את *(et)* indicates an upcoming definite direct object (the heavens) and has no meaning of its own. Therefore, there is no translation.

However, reading the first few words of the Torah as a complete thought, the Rabbis reveal a hidden meaning in et.

In the beginning God created את *(et)*.

את *(Et)* is made up of the first and last letters of the Hebrew alphabet. Et represents the entire Hebrew alphabet, the alephbet, from beginning to end, from aleph to tav.

Rabbi Dov Ber, the Maggid of Mezritch teaches:

> **This is the secret of "In the beginning God created את** *(et).*" **It means: In the beginning, God created the letters of the alephbet from aleph until tav. First, God created the Hebrew letters. And with the letters He created all worlds** (Or Torah, B'reishit).

God's Building Blocks

The Hebrew letters are God's primordial building blocks for all creation.

In Sefer Yetzirah, The Book of Creation, a mystical text attributed to the patriarch Avraham, Hebrew letters are called stones.

Rav Avraham ben David, the Raavad, explains:

> **Like a stone that is quarried from a boulder, so too the letters are quarried from God's name, our Rock** (Raavad, Sefer Yetzirah 4:12).

Sfat Emet explains:

> **The letters are called stones because, just as stones are the foundation of a building, everything was created from the twenty-two letters of the Torah** (Sfat Emet, VaYetzeh תרנ"ז ד"ה ויפגע).

Like one builds a home by combining stones in different ways, God created the world by combining Hebrew letters in different sequences. Each possible combination and permutation of letters brings forth a new and unique creation. For example, combining the three letters א *(aleph)*, ב *(bet)*, and ן *(nun sofit)* creates אבן *(even)* stone. Through combining the Hebrew letters in an almost infinite number of ways, God creates all reality.

> **"Twenty-two Foundation letters: He engraved them, He carved them, He permuted them, He weighed them, He transformed them, And with them, He depicted all that was formed and all that would be formed"** (Aryeh Kaplan, Sefer Yetzirah 2:2).

Sefer Yetzirah calculates the number of creations that can be made from all the permutations of all the letters:

> **Two stones [letters] build 2 houses [creations]. Three stones build 6 houses. Four stones build 24 houses... etc.... seven stones build 5040 houses. From here on, go out and calculate that which the mouth cannot speak and the ear cannot hear** (Aryeh Kaplan, Sefer Yetzirah 4:16).

Scientists study the deep, physical nature of the universe. The sages study the Hebrew letters to discover the divine essence of the universe.

Now we understand the first verse of the Torah this way:

In the beginning God created את *(et)*, the Hebrew letters, and with them He created the heavens and the earth.

God Dwells Inside the Letters

Not only does God create the world with the Hebrew letters, but:

> **The spirituality of the Holy One dwells inside the letters** (Baal Shem Tov, Toldot Yaakov Yosef).

All of creation is made up of God-filled Hebrew letters. This is hinted at in the first four letters of the Hebrew alephbet.

א *(aleph)*

ב *(bet)*

ג *(gimel)*

ד *(dalet)*

In a system called gematria (that I will present shortly), every letter corresponds to a number. Aleph, the first letter in the alephbet, is the number one. It hints to the Oneness of God.

The next three letters, ב *(bet)*, ג *(gimel)*, and ד *(dalet)*, spell the word בגד *(begged)*, which means garment.

א *(Aleph)*, the One God, begins creation by creating and clothing Himself in the בגד *(begged)* garment of the Hebrew alephbet. Then, the God-filled Hebrew letters create the world. By studying creation and the Hebrew letters that enliven it, we come closer to knowing God.

God Spoke the World into Existence

First, God created the Hebrew letters. He combined the letters into words and spoke the world into existence.

And God said: Let there be light, and there was light (B'reishit 1:3).

Remember, saying that God speaks is not literal; it is a metaphor for a spiritual reality.

In our daily morning prayers we acknowledge that God creates with speech:

> **Blessed is the one who spoke, and the world came into being** (Pesukei Dezimrah, Morning Prayer).

The Rabbis teach:

> **With ten utterances the world was created** (Pirkei Avot, *Ethics of the Fathers* 5:1).

The ten utterances are in the beginning of B'reishit. God said: "Let there be light," is one. God said: "Let there be a firmament within the waters," is another. And so on.

Previously we learned that God creates everything by combining Hebrew letters in an infinite number of ways. Now we see that God created the world with ten utterances. Which one is it — ten or infinite? Of course, it is both. It is the letters of the ten utterances combined in infinite ways.

All things are made up of the ten utterances. But they don't articulate all the particulars of creation as the Tanya explains:

> **Individual creatures are not capable of receiving their life force directly from the ten utterances of the Torah, because the life force issuing directly from the ten utterances is far greater than the capacity of the individual creations to receive. They can receive their life force only when it descends, and is progressively diminished, degree by degree** (Sha'ar Hayichud V'haemunah, Chapter 1).

All creation emanates, level by level, from the letters of the original ten divine utterances.

Sustaining the World with Hebrew Letters

God did not create the world with Hebrew letters only in some distant past moment. God continually pours His life force into the Hebrew letters to both create and sustain reality.

> **It is written: Your words, God, are forever positioned in the heavens. The Baal Shem Tov taught that the words and letters that God spoke, "Let there be a firmament within the water, etc."** (B'reishit 1:6), **are positioned forever within the firmament of the heavens, to give them life. As it is written, "The word of our God exists forever** (Isaiah 40:8)**..." Because if the letters would depart, even for a moment, and return to their source, God forbid, all the heavens would be like nothing, as if they had never been, as it was before God said: "Let there be a firmament." And so it is with everything that is created in all the upper and lower worlds. Even in the physical world, and even the inanimate, if the letters of the ten utterances that God spoke would depart, even for a moment, all would immediately return to nothingness** (Tanya, Sha'ar Hayechud V'haemunah, Chapter 1).

Hebrew letters are the essential, constant, divine vitality enlivening everything in creation. Like blood flowing through the body, continually distributing oxygen essential for life, Hebrew letters flow through all of reality, delivering God's vital life force. Without the Hebrew letters, creation ceases to exist.

God is creating the world with Hebrew letters now. The vitality of the breath you are breathing now is from God's speaking the letters נ (*nun*), ש (*shin*), י (*yud*), מ (*mem*), and ה (*heh*) to create and sustain your נשימה *(neshima)* breath. ל *(Lamed)* and ב *(bet)*, לב *(lev)* heart are combining to create your heart and keep it beating.

Letters and Words

Hebrew letters enliven all creation. In this book we will study, in particular, the words and letters of the Torah.

A beautiful source calling us to the study of the words and letters is found in the story of Noah's ark. As the flood begins, God tells Noah:

> **Come into the ark** (B'reishit 7:1).

The Hebrew word for ark is תיבה *(teiva)*. Not everyone knows that תיבה *(teiva)* also means word.

Sfat Emet explains:

> **Come into the teiva means come into the word, into the hidden levels of the letters** (Sfat Emet, Noach תרל״ב ד״ה אא״ז).

Just as God beckons Noah to come into the ark, he beckons us to come into the words and letters of Torah.

Sweet Starlight

We have begun to see that Hebrew is more elevated, powerful, and divinely creative than anything we can fully grasp. To imagine that we are clearly seeing Hebrew with our eyes, or fully understanding it with our minds, is like imagining we are seeing the full radiance of the light of a star at its source. The full light of Hebrew shines in the mind of God. Through Hebrew, God transforms His thoughts and desires for creation into physical reality. When we contemplate the secrets of Hebrew, we are contemplating God's creation.

In many Jewish communities it was traditional to introduce the Hebrew alephbet to young children by writing the letters in honey and inviting the children to lick the sweet letters. This was done, as the Israeli musician Shlomo Bar sings, "so that Torah in the mouth will be sweet like the taste of honey." With sweet letters in their mouths, children

Taste and see that God is good (Psalms 34:9).

4
Playing with Torah

Torah Study Day and Night

By looking deeply into creation, we discover Torah everywhere. Avraham was the first to discover Torah in creation. Even before it was revealed on Mount Sinai, Avraham knew Torah.

> **In truth, even before receiving the Torah, the righteous ones heard the words of the living God in the world, from creation itself** (Sfat Emet, VaYechi תרס״ב ד״ה בפסוק).

> **Avraham comprehended the whole Torah with his own intelligence, even though the Torah hadn't been given yet. Looking inward and outward, he perceived the ways of Torah** (Degel Machane Efraim, Parshat Toldot).

Generations after Avraham, God revealed Torah to the entire Jewish people. From that moment on, Jews have been studying Torah.

Every evening in our prayers we say:

> **We will rejoice in the words of Your Torah and Your mitzvahs forever, because they are our life and the length of our days, and we will contemplate them day and night** (Shma, Evening Prayer).

We study Torah day and night because Torah is our life.

ONE OF MY GREATEST TORAH teachers is Rav Ben Yishai. He uses a metaphor to describe our vital connection to Torah: If a person goes under water unaided, he can survive for only a few minutes. But if a person takes oxygen with him, he can stay under water longer. Like this, when we descend into the created world, we need to be connected to oxygen from the higher world in order to live. That oxygen is Torah. Connecting ourselves to Torah day and night is as essential to our life as breathing.

Rav Ben Yishai is one of the most alive people I know. When he teaches Torah he looks like a soaring eagle. He raises his arms out to the sides of his body and lifts them up like mighty wings. My soul soars with him in his classes.

Rav Ben Yishai's personal history makes his elevating power utterly remarkable. He lived through the unthinkable loss of his daughter, Ruth, his son-in-law, Udi, and three of his grandchildren, Hadas, Elad, and Yoav, who were all murdered in a terror attack in Israel. He and his wife, Tali, also a remarkably positive and joyful Torah teacher, have been raising the three surviving grandchildren, Tamar, Roi, and Yishai, since the attack. When Rav Ben Yishai teaches that Torah is our oxygen in a world that would otherwise be deadly, he is speaking from personal experience. May his loving Torah continue to elevate and bless the world.

Transforming Study to Play

Jews have been studying Torah day and night for thousands of years — not because we are slow learners, but because there are endlessly deepening levels of meaning in Torah.

We read many times in the Torah:

And God spoke to Moses saying...

The Rabbis ask why it is necessary to add the word "saying". It could easily just say: And God spoke to Moses.

Rabbeinu Bachaye teaches that "God spoke" is the revealed meaning of Torah, and "saying" is the concealed meaning.

All the words of Torah have revealed and concealed meanings (Rebbeinu Bachaye, Shmot 13:1).

The multilevel meanings of Torah are also hinted at in the words:

God spoke one, and I heard two (Psalms 62:12).

From every story, every word, and every letter that God speaks in the Torah we can hear many things.

As we have seen, the Ramak teaches that there are four levels of Torah study: the stories, the commandments, the Kabbalah, and the Hebrew letters. The four levels of Torah study are also often described as פרדס *(pardes)* an orchard. Pardes is an acronym for פשט *(pshat)* simple, literal; רמז *(remez)* hint; דרש *(drash)* interpretation based on comparison with other verses of the Torah; and סוד *(sod)* secret, essence. Torah is interpreted on all these levels.

An orchard is an appropriate metaphor for Torah. Rabbi Yaakov Leiner, the Beit Yaakov, teaches that, with the giving of Torah, the meaning of creation began to be revealed. He compares creation to an unripe fruit — without taste, without meaning. The giving of Torah is the ripening of the fruit of creation. The more we attend to the orchard through study and practice, the more tastes we discover and the sweeter the fruit becomes (Beit Yaakov, Yitro 126).

Our sages have taught many rules for Torah study. In the study of Halacha (Jewish law), for example, Rabbi Yishmael articulated thirteen rules. In this book I offer some rules for Torah study that I have encountered in my years of learning traditional texts. I call these Rules of Play. They describe playful ways our sages entered all the levels of the pardes to taste the ripening fruits of Torah.

Just as Torah was a source of delight and play for God before creation, it is meant to be a source of delight and play now in creation. We imitate God by playing with Torah. It is play of the highest order, a play that has the power to transform mourning into dancing and darkness into light.

As Torah herself says:

> **I play on the earth and my delight is with the sons of man**
> (Proverbs 8:31).

The following Rules of Play bring delight to my Torah study, to this book, and to my life.

Rules of Play

1. **Beginnings contain the whole.** The first appearance of a word in the Torah is like a fertile seed from which all its meanings grow. Connect any word you are studying back to its beginnings to understand more. The first word in the Torah, בראשית (B'reishit), contains the whole Torah.

2. **Know that every word in the Torah has something to teach.** The word את (et) is a great example of this. Throughout this book we will discover multileveled meanings of many words in Torah.

3. **Expand a word by dividing it into two or more parts.** The name שרי (Sarai), read as שר י (sar yud), has much to tell.

4. **See a word as an acronym.** The letters in בראשית (b'reishit) are an acronym for בראשונה ראה אלוקים שיקבלו ישראל תורה (b'rishonah raah Elokim sheyikablu Yisrael Torah) in the beginning God saw that Israel would receive Torah.

5. **Notice when words repeat and understand that repetition teaches something new.** The repetition of the word listen in אם שמוע תשמעו (im shamoa tishmeu) does not just emphasize the importance of listening.

6. **When words are built with the same sequence of letters, consider how they are related and how they enhance each other's meanings.** The word עקרה (akara) means barren. The word עיקר (ikar) means essential. The word לעקור (la'akor) means to uproot.

7. **Rearrange the letters and see what other words you can make.** One of the many ways בראשית (b'reishit) can be rearranged is into תבא שרי (tavo Sarai) Sarai is coming.

8. **Draw understanding from the shapes of the Hebrew letters.** Their form reflects their wisdom. The shape of the letter yud contains secrets of creation and the Jewish soul.

9. **The first letter of a word can call to mind other words that begin with that letter.** See if you can find thematic connections between those words. The bet of b'reishit is also the first letter of bracha, blessing.

10. **A part of a verse can be read as an independent thought.** Punctuate a Torah verse differently to discover additional meanings. "In the beginning God created the heavens and the earth" can be read as "In the beginning, God created et."

11. **Every Hebrew letter also corresponds to a number.** Aleph is 1, bet is 2, yud is 10, kaf is 20, lamed is 30, kuf is 100, resh is 200, shin is 300, tav is 400. The gematria of a word is the sum of its letter-numbers. Compare words that share the same gematria. They often have a meaningful and sometimes surprising relationship. חכמה *(Chochmah)* wisdom and גלם *(gelem)* raw material both have the gematria of 73.

12. **Know that the gematria of even a single letter has meaning.** Aleph is 1, hinting at God's oneness.

13. **All letters other than yud are made up of a combination of letters.** Consider the meaning of all parts of a letter. The letter bet is made up of the letters dalet and vav.

14. **Kabbalah teaches that the first letter of the Hebrew alephbet, aleph, can be exchanged with the last letter, tav; the second letter, bet, can be exchanged with the second-to-last letter, shin, etc.** This is called אתבש *(atbash)*. By exchanging letters with atbash we can uncover new meanings of words. Through atbash the word mitzvah reveals the hidden essence of mitzvahs.

15. **Juxtaposition of words and stories is never random in the Torah.** Look for hinted meanings between words and stories that are next to each other in the text. Sarah and Avraham begin their journey to the Land of Israel right after we hear that Sarah is barren.

16. **Everything that is written in the Torah has enduring relevance.** Connect what you learn in torah to your own life.

Being a Student

Before I present two more rules of play, we need to understand the concept of תלמיד חכם *(talmid chacham)*. It means a wise student. It also means a student of a wise teacher.

These two meanings are inseparable. One cannot be a wise student of Torah unless one is learning from a wise teacher.

> **The wise one must always add to his wisdom and learn from someone greater than himself. As well, he must teach someone who knows less than himself** (Sfat Emet, Korach תרס"ד ד"ה במדרש).

Torah is like a waterfall. To be wise, one must become a part of the waterfall, receiving Torah from wise teachers and passing it on to others. If one is not part of the flow of wisdom, one cannot be called wise.

Transmission of wisdom is the theme of the first mishna of Pirkei Avot, *Ethics of the Fathers.*

Moses received Torah from Sinai, and transmitted it to Joshua, and Joshua transmitted it to the elders, and the elders transmitted it to the prophets, and the prophets transmitted it to the men of the Great Assembly (Pirkei Avot, *Ethics of the Fathers 1:1*).

All Torah sages, past and present, are students of wise teachers. The sages always acknowledge and give credit to the wisdom of their teachers. Sfat Emet quotes his revered and beloved grandfather in almost every one of his teachings. You will never find a Sfat Emet teaching that does not include a reference to a sage or to a passage from one of the many books of Torah.

In addition to always learning from a teacher, Torah students traditionally learn with a study partner, called a חברותא *(chevruta)*. The words חבר *(chaver)* friend and חיבור *(chibur)* connection are in the word chevruta. Immersed together in Torah, chevruta partners connect in soulful friendship.

Solitary study and contemplation also play a precious part in Torah study. Some of the greatest sages spent decades learning and writing in solitude. However, no great Torah scholar has learned only in solitude.

The Torah does not command us to be wise. It does, however, command us to study. I learned from my teacher, colleague, and friend Arthur Kurzweil that in the world of Torah study, it is a greater compliment to call someone a student than to call them wise.

Deeply Rooted Renewal

Is there room for חידושים (*chidushim*) new ideas in this tradition that defines wisdom as something received from teachers? There are many different and often conflicting answers to this question.

One answer can be extracted from Rashi's explanation of the words:

> **And it will be, if you שמע תשמעו (shamoa tishmeu) listen listen to the commandments that I command you this day, to love the Lord your God with all your heart and with all your soul** (D'varim 11:13).

The word listen is repeated twice. As we learned in our rules of play, when words repeat in the Torah, the repetition teaches something new. What new thing do we learn from the repetition of the word listen?

Rashi says:

> **שמע *(Shamoa)* If you listen to what is old, תשמעו *(tishmeu)* you will hear the new** (Rashi, D'varim 11:13).

According to Rashi, there is room for discovering new insights in the Torah. New wisdom comes from deep immersion in established wisdom. Like a new leaf growing out of an old, well-rooted tree, new Torah insights grow from deep roots.

The rules of play I offer in this book are meant to be used in the context of the tradition of learning from the wise. Therefore, an essential rule of play is:

17. Remember to connect your Torah play to the great tradition of learning from wise teachers.

Rabbi Abraham Isaac HaCohen Kook, HaRav Kook, whose new Torah insights were deeply rooted in the soil of tradition, understood that there is no easily defined answer to the question of how far we can go with our new insights in Torah and still call it Torah.

> Who can tell us that we can only go until here? Who can give us the clear measurements that until here is the boundary of Torah and the expression of new ideas, but from here onward you have already passed the limit and entered into the experience of the individual, expressed in songs, writings, visions, ideas, logic, but they are not words of Torah. Oy! How hard is the spiritual life and how complicated its powerful ways! Who can make rules here?! Divine assistance here is clearly needed (Chadarav, page 112).

Following in the footsteps of HaRav Kook, the ultimate rule of play is:

18. Ask for divine assistance when you play with the fire of Torah.

5
Playing with B'reishit

The First Letter

The first rule of play is: Beginnings contain the whole. The first appearance of a word in the Torah is like a fertile seed from which all its meanings grow.

> All five books of the Torah are included within the one book of B'reishit, and the entire book of B'reishit is included within the portion of B'reishit, and the whole portion of B'reishit is included within the first verse of B'reishit, and the first verse of B'reishit is included within the word B'reishit, and the word B'reishit is included within the letter bet of the word B'reishit, and the letter bet of the word B'reishit is included within the point that is within the letter bet of the word B'reishit (Stan Tenen, *The Alphabet that Changed the World*, quoting the Rebbe of Tosh, page 11).

We begin our playful study with the first letter of the Torah:

(Bet)

It is well known that, when words are translated, much is lost. This is true for any language, but translating the Hebrew of the Torah is a problem of an entirely different magnitude.

For example, the letter ב *(bet)* at the beginning of a Hebrew word is a preposition literally meaning with, in, or through. But if we only understand bet literally, we lose a lot.

- We have lost the opportunity to perceive hints in the letter: The Midrash asks, why did the Torah start with bet? It answers that ב implies ברכה *(bracha)* blessing, teaching us that, from the very beginning, the world is created for the purpose of blessing.

- We have the lost the word בית *(bayit)* home, which is the letter bet spelled out. Creation is a home for human beings and God.

- We have lost the shape of the ב, which is closed above, below, and behind and open in the front. (Remember, Hebrew is written from right to left.) Although we cannot always see what is above, below, or behind us, the front door of our lives is always open. The shape of the ב beckons us to move forward.

- We have lost the pointers on the right and left of the letter. The left pointer points up, hinting that God above created this world. The right points back to the hidden first letter, saying that God's name is Aleph, One (Midrash Rabbah, B'reishit 1).

- We have lost the gematria of bet — two — which symbolizes the paradox that God, who is and remains eternally One, has created a world of plurality.

- We have lost the letters that make up the shape of the letter ב — an upright ד *(dalet)* and a horizontal ו *(vav)*. Kabbalah teaches that dalet and vav represent feminine and masculine. The duality of feminine and masculine is essential to creation.

- We have lost the gematria of bet's component letters — ד *(dalet)* 4 and ו *(vav)* 6 which added together make 10. Ten is the letter י *(yud)*. We will speak about yud at great length later.

This is just a taste of what is hidden in the letter bet. The book *Why the Torah Begins with the Letter Bet*, by Michael J. Alter, is more than 300 pages long!

> **So much is lost in translation. No wonder the Rabbis taught: On the eighth of Tevet, during the days of King Ptolemy, the Torah was translated into Greek, and three days of darkness came into the world** (Shulchan Aruch, Orach Chayyim, Hilchot Ta'anit).

Even though so much is lost in translation, we translate in order to spread the blessings of Torah to a world that is not fluent in Hebrew.

To reopen the shutters closed by translation, and to let in the light of a fuller understanding, I will often give multiple meanings of Hebrew words in this book.

The First Word

We continue our playful Torah study with the first word of the Torah.

בראשית *(B'reishit)* ... (B'reishit 1:1).

This word says nothing but דרשני *(darsheyni)* **explain me, ask of me, investigate me, interpret me** (Rashi, B'reishit 1:1).

The most common translation of בראשית *(b'reishit)* is

ב *(b')* in

ראשית *(reishit)* the beginning

But it means much more. In just one kabbalistic text, Tikunei HaZohar, there are seventy commentaries on the word b'reishit. Delving into this word, the sages reveal glimpses of divine secrets and the purpose of creation. Using our rules of play, I offer a few insights, a beginning glimpse.

Beginning with Torah

In the Midrash we saw that God creates the world with Torah. This idea is also found in the first word of the Torah.

ב *(b')* with

ראשית *(reishit)*

> **With reishit God created the heavens and the earth** (B'reishit 1:1).

What is reishit? As well as meaning beginning, the Midrash teaches:

> **Reishit is Torah** (Midrash Rabbah, B'reishit 1:1).

This is based on the verse in Proverbs, where Torah itself speaks:

> **God created me** ראשית *(reishit)*, **(I am) the beginning of His ways** (Proverbs 8:22).

Now we see:

With Torah, God created the heavens and the earth.

Beginning with Israel

We have begun to glimpse the essential role of Torah in creation. Israel also has an essential role in creation. This also is found in the word b'reishit.

The prophet Jeremiah describes Israel as God's reishit.

> **Israel is holy to God, reishit / the first of his harvest** (Jeremiah 2:3).

So, we can say:

With Israel, God created the heavens and the earth.

What does it mean that God created the heavens and earth with Israel? What do we mean by Israel? Do we mean the people Israel? After all, it is twenty generations from the time of Adam and Eve until the appearance of the first father and mother of the Jewish people, Sarah and Avraham. And it is not until later that the people are called Israel.

The Rabbis of the Midrash help solve this puzzle:

> **There are six things that preceded the creation of the world. Some of those were created, and some were in (God's) thought to create. Torah and the Throne of Glory were created... The Patriarchs and Matriarchs of the Jewish people, and Israel, and the Temple, and the name of the Messiah were in God's thoughts** (Midrash Rabbah, B'reishit 1:4).

The Rabbis present different opinions about which was the first of God's thoughts.

> **Rav Huna in the name of Rabbi Yermiah, in the name of Rav Shmuel, the son of Rav Itzchak said: The thought of Israel preceded everything** (Midrash Rabbah, B'reishit 1:4).

Rabbi Eliyahu de Vidas explains what the thought of Israel is:

> **The root of the soul of Israel preceded the world** (Reishit Chochmah, Shaar HaKedusha, Chapter 1).

In the mysterious realm before creation, the root of the soul of Israel was God's original thought.

Weaving these b'reishit teachings together, we expand the first verse of Torah to say:

With the root of the soul of Israel in His thoughts, God created the heavens and the earth.

Why Create with Torah and Israel?

> **Through Torah and Israel, who are reishit, the essential purpose of creation is clarified** (Sfat Emet, Succoth תרס״ב ד״ה המשך).

Rabbi Moses Chayim Luzzato, the Ramchal, presents a foundational teaching on the purpose of creation:

> **God's purpose in creation is to bestow His good** (Derech HaShem, Part 1).

God gives His goodness through Torah, which is called good.

> **A good teaching I have given to you, My Torah, do not abandon it** (Proverbs 4:2).

> **Torah is the essence of goodness for a person** (Sfat Emet, B'reishit תרל״ד ד״ה במדרש).

Torah is both the essence of God's goodness and the way that goodness is carried to all creation. In order to give of His goodness, God needs a creation capable of receiving it. That creation is the people of Israel.

> **The Children of Israel are capable of receiving Torah** (Sfat Emet, Yitro תרמ"ז ד"ה במדרש).

Israel's capacity to receive Torah is playfully hiding in an acronym of the word בראשית *(b'reishit).*

> **בראשונה ראה אלוקים שיקבלו ישראל תורה,** *(b'rishonah raah Elokim sheyikablu Yisrael Torah)* **In the beginning God saw that Israel would receive Torah** (Baal HaTurim, B'reishit 1).

The Gemara says:

> **The good one will come and receive good from The Good, for the good. The good one will come. This is Moses, as it is written: And she saw that he was good** (Shmot 2:2).
>
> **And receive good. This is the Torah, as it is written: A good teaching I have given you** (Proverbs 3:18).
>
> **From The Good. This is the Holy One, as it is written: God is good to all** (Psalms 145:9).
>
> **For the good. This is Israel, as it is written: God has given good to the good** (Psalms 125:4 and Babylonian Talmud, Menachot 53b).

Sfat Emet repeatedly teaches that Torah is given to Israel for the sake of bringing goodness to the whole world.

> **The Torah was meant to be revealed to the whole world. For this purpose the world was created. But the world was not prepared to receive it** (Sfat Emet, Yitro תרמ"ז ד"ה במדרש).

Israel has the potential to draw blessing down for the whole world. Every person of Israel must understand, in his heart, that everything has been given into his hands and that he should do his part in bringing goodness to the world. It is dependent on him (Sfat Emet, Re'eh תר"מ ד"ה במדרש).

With Torah, God gives His goodness, through Israel, to His creation.

Continually Sustaining the World with Torah and Israel

Torah and Israel were essential at the beginning of God's creating. They are also essential for sustaining creation.

We find this hinted in the words "the sixth day," in the creation story. The sixth day is the only day of creation where the definite article ה *(hey)* the is used:

> **And there was evening and there was morning the sixth day** (B'reishit 1:31).

The second day is called "second day." The third day is called "third day," etc. (The first day is called "day one," which is a different topic entirely.)

> **Rabbi Shimon Ben LaKish taught: Why does it say in the creation story, day one, second day, third day, fourth day, fifth day, ה** *(hey)* **the sixth day? Why is there the extra ה** *(hey)* **the? This teaches that the Holy One made a condition with all of creation and said: If Israel will receive the Torah, which has in it five books, it will be good. If not, I am returning you to void and chaos** (Midrash Tanchuma 1).

ה *(Hey)* is **5** in gematria. The hey in the sixth day hints to the חומש *(Chumash)* the Five Books of Moses.

Also, the words "the sixth day" hint to the particular future sixth day of the month of Sivan, the day God gives the Torah to the Jewish people.

> **All was dependent and waiting for the sixth day, the sixth of Sivan, the day of the giving of the Torah** (Rashi, B'reishit 1:31).

The Talmud teaches that all creation depends on the sixth day of Sivan, on Israel receiving the Torah. Without this all would return to void and chaos.

> **It is God's will to create a human being who is occupied with Torah. Everyone who contemplates and occupies himself with Torah keeps the whole world in existence. The Holy One looks into the Torah and creates the world, and the human being looks into the Torah and keeps the world in existence. What a great merit it is to be a human being occupied with Torah** (Zohar 2:161b)!

Torah is the essential divine breath of all creation. Just like a human being cannot exist without breath, the world cannot exist without someone occupied with Torah. Because of this there is a custom of ensuring that there are at least a few people learning Torah at all times, to ensure the continued existence of the world.

Weaving these meanings into one more expanding understanding of the first Torah verse, we have:

Through Israel, God gives His goodness, Torah, creating and sustaining the heavens and the earth.

Torah is Hiding in All of Creation

Since the world is created and sustained by Torah, it follows that, when we look into the world we should always discover Torah.

> **There is illumination from Torah in everything, because the Holy One created the world with Torah** (Sfat Emet, Chukat תרל״א ד״ה בזוהר).

It is safe to say that most human beings do not see Torah in everything. If there is illumination from Torah in everything, why doesn't everyone see Torah everywhere? Because it is hidden.

> **When the world was created, the Torah was immediately hidden in the world. Therefore, it is not recognized or known, and we need to find the illumination of the Torah that is hidden in creation** (Sfat Emet, Chukat תרל״א ד״ה בזוהר).

The Torah does not simply say: "With Torah and Israel, God created the heavens and the earth." Rather, it hides Torah and Israel in the word b'reishit, teaching us that Torah and Israel have been hidden in the world since the first moment of creation. It is the purpose of the people of Israel to receive the good light of Torah and reveal it to the world.

We have begun to glimpse the beginning of what is hidden in בראשית *(b'reishit)* in the beginning.

6
Beginning with Sarah and Avraham

Early Sightings

The divine thought of Israel begins to reveal itself in creation with Sarah and Avraham. We first encounter Sarah and Avraham as Sarai and Avram early in the book of B'reishit.

> **And Terach lived seventy years, and he gave birth to Avram, to Nachor and to Charan** (B'reishit 11:26). **And Avram and Nachor took for themselves wives, the name of the wife of Avram was Sarai.... And Sarai was barren, she had no child** (B'reishit 11:29-30).

Later in the story, God changes their names to Sarah and Avraham.

On another level of reading, we find Sarah and Avraham much earlier. Moti Golan, a Torah teacher in Jerusalem, showed me where Sarai is playfully hiding in the first word of Torah.

Rearranging the letters of ב ר א ש י ת we have:

תבא שרי *(tavo Sarai)* Sarai will come.

Given the idea that beginnings contain the whole, we should not be too surprised to find Sarah peering out at us from the first word of Torah. God had Sarah in mind from the beginning of creation.

Creating the World with Avraham

Avraham's name is also hidden early in the Torah.

> **These are the generations of the heavens and the earth** בהבראם *(b'hibaram)* **when they were created** (B'reishit 2:4).

Rearranging the letters of ב ה ב ר א ם reveals:

> ב א ב ר ה ם *(b'Avraham)* **with Avraham** (Midrash Rabbah, B'reishit 12:9).

We expand our understanding of the verse this way:

These are the generations of the heavens and earth when He created them with Avraham in mind.

Both Sarah and Avraham are hidden in Hebrew words at the beginning of creation.

Ancient Roots – Soul Mirrors

Avraham and Sarah, Yitzchak and Rivka, Yaakov, Rachel, and Leah — the first three generations of ancestors of the Jewish people — are called the Avot.

I HAVE LEARNED MOST ABOUT the Avot from my teacher in Jerusalem, Nurit G'al Dor. Nurit is a passionate and powerful teacher. I am riveted by the crystal clarity of her insights, exhilarated by the love for Torah that burns in her words, and moved to tears by her faith. In her voice, in her eyes, I hear and see the fiery Hebrew letters that I fell in love with as a little girl.

Nurit often closes her eyes when she teaches, appearing to be in direct conversation with our elevated ancestors. She is not just passing on ideas she has heard from others. She knows Sarah and Avraham not as distant, biblical characters, but as living wellsprings for her faith in God and the Jewish people.

In her words:

> **The Avot are our ancient roots, and in their lives is embedded the purpose of the Jewish people. In our encounter with them, we can come to know what God wants from us — the holy and the elevated** (Zera Avraham Ohavi, page 44).

Almost two thousand years ago, the Rabbis of the Talmud wrote:

> **In the future, the Holy One will say to Israel: Go to your Avot, and they will instruct you** (Babylonian Talmud, Shabbat 89b).

Nurit G'al Dor explains what is meant by "in the future":

> **Even though throughout history it was always important to study the book of B'reishit (which includes the stories of the Avot), in the future, at the time of returning to Zion, and the ingathering of the exiles, it will have even greater importance** (Zera Avraham Ohavi, page 45).

Our Ancient Future Land

That future time is now. The Jewish people are returning to Zion from exiles that scattered them to the four corners of the earth: the Assyrian exile of the ten tribes in 740 BCE, the Babylonian exile after the destruction of the first Temple in 586 BCE, and the Roman exile following the destruction of the second Temple in 70 CE.

The return of a people to their land after such extended and far-flung exiles is an unprecedented phenomenon in human history. Exile usually leads to assimilation. No exiled nation has ever returned to their native land, except for the Jews. In this unprecedented ingathering of exiles, Jews are returning to Israel from every continent.

The Dalai Lama, the spiritual leader of the exiled Tibetan Buddhist people, recognized the miracle of the Jewish people's survival in exile. He sent out an invitation to a wide range of Rabbis and Jewish scholars asking them to reveal their secret. The book *The Jew in the Lotus* by Roger Kamenetz presents many of those answers.

As I see it, our survival is in part due to our faith in God's promise to the Jewish people. We have never stopped praying to return to our land. Three times a day, during the thousands of years of exile, and continuing today, we pray:

> **Blow the great shofar for our freedom and lift up a banner to quickly gather our exiles, and gather us together from the four corners of the earth to our land** (Amidah prayer).

It is ultimately a testament to the faithfulness of God to Israel. Moses, the greatest prophet, says:

> **Even if you are scattered to the ends of the heavens, the Lord, your God, will gather you from there, and from there He will take you. And the Lord, your God, will bring you to the land that your ancestors inherited, and you will inherit it, and He will do good for you, and make you more numerous than your ancestors** (D'varim 30:4-5).

THIS MIRACULOUS INGATHERING INCLUDES ME. It includes my husband, Jonathan, and my cousins, Becca and Danny. And most recently, my sister and brother-in-law, Laura and Mark, who came to Israel after a thirteen-year sailing expedition in which they circumnavigated the planet — they literally came from the four corners of the earth!

I did not include my daughter, Kalya, in this list of family members because she is a sabra. Sabra is the word for someone born in Israel. Israelis are called sabras because they have the reputation of being prickly on the outside and sweet on the inside, like the fruit of the sabra cactus.

For years I have loved describing Kalya as the first sabra in our family in two thousand years. What a miracle! Recently I have realized that perhaps my story is even more amazing. I live in a time when ancient prophesies that the Jews would return to their land are coming true. And I am one of those returnees. My story is written in the prophet Jeremiah's words describing God bringing his exiled children back to their land.

> **I took you, one from a city and two from a family, and I brought you to Zion** (Jeremiah 3:14).

I came back to Israel "one from a city" — I alone, from the midst of a very large family. Whenever I am asked why I moved to Israel, I always say my soul brought me here. It is that simple and that deep. What else could take me so far from my wonderful family? Forty years later, with my sister and brother-in-law miraculously making aliyah, the second half of the verse has also come true. Aliyah means going up. It is the word used for moving to Israel. Now God has brought back "two from a family" — two from my family!

On my first trip to Israel, I was fortunate to meet Golda Meir, the fourth Prime Minister of Israel, and hear her speak. About the Jews who were not returning to Israel, she said:

> **I don't understand why Jews are so unselfish. For thousands of years our people have longed to return home to Israel. Why do they not take what we have always dreamed of?**
> (Golda Meir in a private lecture in Jerusalem, 1977)

At that moment I knew I would make aliyah. I knew I would raise myself up to the vision of the Jewish people that began with Sarah and Avraham.

Why Study Avraham and Sarah Now?

The first Jews to go up to the Land of Israel were Sarah and Avraham. The first words God said to Avraham were:

> **Go forth from your land and from your birthplace and from your father's home to the land that I will show you**
> (B'reishit 12:1).

From that time on, Avraham and Sarah's lives and the lives of their descendants have been inextricably bound up with the Land of Israel, either because they were living in the land or because they were in exile, longing to return.

Sfat Emet teaches that when we are in exile we are separated from the roots of our existence. When we are separated from our roots in the Land of Israel we are separated from our roots in our ancestors. Returning to the land, we must also return to our Avot.

> **Returning to the Avot is redemption. When this happens, the Children of Israel will be renewed like a new creation. Not only this, but the whole world will be renewed when the light of the Avot is awakened in Israel** (Sfat Emet, Bo תרס"א ד"ה במדרש).

Rav Kook also teaches that the way back to our holy nature after exile is through deep immersion in the study of the Avot:

> **What will guide us to a spiritual restoration will be a return to our holy nature, a powerful holding on to the characteristics of the Avot. They are the foundations of our holy legacy** (Ein Ayah, Shabbat Part 2).

We, the Jewish people, are now returning to our land and waking up to the light of the Avot. We dive now into the study of the Avot. We begin with their soul.

We are not so used to talking about the soul. Rabbi Abraham Joshua Heschel says that ultimate questions about the soul are the object of modern man's favorite unawareness.

> **"Our theories will go awry, will all throw dust into our eyes, unless we dare to confront not only the world, but the soul as well"** (Man is Not Alone, page 191).

In Torah, especially in Chassidut and Kabbalah, the soul is the favorite subject of awareness.

One Secret Timeless Soul

The stories of the Avot foreshadow the future of the Jewish people.

> **The actions of the Avot are a sign for their children. That is why the text elaborates the stories of their journeys, the digging of the wells, and all the other events. One should not think that these things are superfluous. All of them teach about the future** (Ramban, B'reishit 12:6).

HOW CAN IT BE THAT Sarah and Avraham's lives foreshadow the future of the Jewish people? How can it be that in their story, which began in ancient Mesopotamia around 1500 BCE, I see my story, which began in Saint Paul, Minnesota, in 1959 CE? How can it be that I heard God's words to Avraham — "Go to the land that I will show you" — echoing in the words of my youth group leader: "Are you going on the USY Israel Pilgrimage next summer?"

To understand, we must know something about Sarah and Avraham's soul. Speaking about both Sarah and Avraham, the prophet Isaiah says:

> **I called him One** (Isaiah 51:2).

Because Isaiah is speaking about both Sarah and Avraham, it would have made more sense to say: I called them One. Nurit G'al Dor explains:

> **Sarah and Avraham are more unified than any man and woman in history. Therefore, in talking about them, God says: "I have called him One," because Sarah and Avraham are one. They exist as one being, one body and one soul. The Holy One gave Sarah and Avraham a unique name, One, because their soul is unified in its purpose of revealing God's goodness to the whole world** (Zera Avraham Ohavi, pages 44-45).

With Sarah and Avraham, a new kind of being comes into the world: two people who exist as one body and soul, whose deepest desire is to reveal the divine good in all reality, throughout all time. Their unified soul and its longing to elevate reality is the soul of the Jewish people. Beginnings contain the whole: The first unified Jewish soul, like a seed, contains all future Jewish souls.

The unified soul of Sarah and Avraham is our spiritual inheritance. We, the Jewish people, also exist as one body and one soul. The Zohar speaks of רזא דאחד *(razah d'echad)* the secret of oneness. This is God's oneness. Razah d'echad is reflected in the world in the Jewish soul, the soul that was in God's thoughts before creation. It is alive today. It is timeless.

> **The righteous ones are called alive even after they have passed away, because their souls illuminate the world forever** (Sfat Emet, Chayyei Sarah תרנ"א ד"ה במדרש).

The study of Sarah and Avraham is not the study of ordinary people or even the study of spiritual giants who lived and died in the ancient past. It is an encounter with an illuminating, living soul. Their soul is a mirror for our soul, in which we see the purpose of our own lives reflected.

Sarah – The First Barren Mother

And now we turn to the life of Sarah.

> **And Avram and Nachor took for themselves wives, the name of the wife of Avram was Sarai.... And Sarai was barren, she had no child** (B'reishit 11:29-30).

There is much in these opening verses that sets Sarah apart from everything that precedes her. Before Sarah, the verse "and he fathered sons and daughters" appears over and over. In these verses, there is almost no mention of the mothers of these sons and daughters. Also, from the time of creation until Sarah, there are no infertility stories. The opposite is true — fertility is the norm in the first twenty generations. With Sarah, natural fertility comes to a sudden halt.

From her first appearance, Sarah is exceptional. Not only is she mentioned by name, but she is the first barren woman in a very fertile world. She is the first, but by no means the last. All four matriarchs of the Jewish people — Sarah, Rivka, Leah, and Rachel — were barren for a time.

> **And Yitzchak pleaded with the Lord in the presence of his wife, because she was barren, and God responded to him, and Rivka his wife became pregnant** (B'reishit 25:21).

The Torah does not explicitly say that Leah, who became the mother of seven children, was initially barren. But her barrenness is hinted at in the verse:

> **And God saw that Leah was hated and He opened her womb** (B'reishit 29:31).

From the words: "He opened her womb," our sages understand that it had been closed.

The Torah is explicit about Rachel:

> **And Rachel was barren** (B'reishit 29:31).

Other women in the Torah were barren for a time — such as the mother of Samson, and Hannah, the mother of the prophet Samuel.

Could it be that all the mothers of the Jewish people just happened to have fertility problems? Or is something deeper about being barren peeking out from under the surface of the text?

The Root of עֲקָרָה Akara

And Sarai was עֲקָרָה *(akara)* barren, she had no child (B'reishit 11:30).

Since it says "and Sarai was barren," don't we already know that "she had no child"? Yes, of course we know. The repetition alerts us to look for deeper meaning here. We find additional layers of meaning not only in the repetition, but in the word akara itself.

Three of the letters in עֲקָרָה *(akara)* — ayin kuf reish — are the root of the verb לַעֲקוֹר *(la'akor)* to uproot.

What is the purpose of uprooting something? In a garden we pull up old roots because the seasons have changed and it is time to grow something new. We uproot sick plants that could harm other plants. We uproot in order to allow new things to grow.

The letters ayin kuf reish are also found in the word עִיקָר *(ikar)* essential.

"And Sarah was akara" means more than "Sarah was barren." The word akara reveals her essence. Sarah was herself an uprooter. She uprooted the prevailing ways of understanding and experiencing life to make room for an essential new way.

God's Role in the Birth of Yitzchak

Before Sarah, God's involvement in birth was hidden, but God's involvement in Yitzchak's birth was revealed at every stage. Decades before Yitzchak was conceived, God revealed to Avraham that he would be the father of a great nation. God promised children to Avraham many times during those long barren years.

> **I will make your offspring as the dust of the earth, so that if one can count the dust of the earth, then your offspring too can be counted** (B'reishit 13:16).

> **And He took him outside and He said, Look toward heaven and count the stars, if you are able to count them, and He said to him, this is how your offspring will be** (B'reishit 15:5).

> **I will make you exceedingly fertile, and make nations of you, and kings shall come forth from you** (B'reishit 17:6).

How much faith Avraham and Sarah must have had to believe God's promises of a child while, year after year, Sarah remained childless. Avraham was one hundred years old and Sarah was ninety when God told Avraham:

> **Sarah, your wife, will bear you a son, and you will call him Yitzchak** (B'reishit 17:19).

> **And I will bless her, and I will give you a son from her** (B'reishit 17:16).

The biological impossibility of Sarah bearing a child highlights God's revealed intervention.

> **And Sarah and Avraham were old, advanced in years, Sarah had ceased having her period as women do** (B'reishit 18:11).

When the angels of God told Avraham that Sarah would have a child, Sarah laughed. In response, God says to Avraham:

> Why did Sarah laugh, saying, Will I give birth, seeing that I have grown old? Is anything too wondrous for God? I will return to you next year at this appointed time and Sarah will have a son (B'reishit 18:13-14).

> And God remembered Sarah, as He had said, and He did to Sarah as He had spoken. And Sarah became pregnant and gave birth to a son to Avraham in his old age, at the appointed time that God had spoken (B'reishit 21:1-2).

Sarah knew in every cell of her ninety-year-old body that the only reason she birthed Yitzchak was because God had stepped in. The story of Sarah giving birth in her tenth decade is the first God-revealing birth story in the Torah. All the mothers that preceded Sarah were not forced, through the trial of infertility, to see God's involvement in the birth of their babies.

The Garden of the Matriarchs

Following Sarah, God's essential role is revealed in the pregnancies of all the matriarchs. They all became uprooters because they themselves had been uprooted. Their barrenness uprooted them from life in the naturally fertile garden of all women who preceded them. It planted them in the garden of faith. Their powerful desire for children made them penetrate through the surface of reality to the essential source of reality — to God.

Revealing God to the World

Beginning with Yitzchak, all the birth stories of the Jewish people bear witness to God. Just as children come from God, everything comes from God. Our birth stories foreshadow our purpose: to root all reality in God.

> **In everything and in every place there is life from God.... A person needs to be a witness to clarify and testify that everything is from God** (Sfat Emet, B'chukotai תרל"ב ד"ה במדרש).

Consider the words of Rabbi Mordechai of Chernobyl testifying to God in all reality:

> **He creates all upper and lower worlds. He fills all worlds. He surrounds all worlds. He maintains all worlds. He is above all worlds. He is under all worlds. He is within all worlds.... We need to believe with complete and strong faith that there is no place empty of God, and His glory is in each and every thing, and His reign is in all realms, even in the outer shells of reality, and He pours His abundance and existence into everything, and if His abundance and life force would depart even for a moment from anything, that thing would be void and chaos** (Likutei Torah, Hadracha bet).

My Connection to Sarah

I FIRST BEGAN TO PAY attention to the story of Sarah when I was in my mid-twenties. I was living in Israel, in a religious community, ready and longing to get married and have a child. I was having a terribly hard time finding a husband. Much like

Sarah, I was surrounded by a lot of people who seemed to me to be easily giving birth to sons and daughters. Year after year passed as I went jealously to another wedding, another brit (circumcision ceremony), another baby naming. Year after year, I went to my friends' children's birthday parties and watched them play with their new brothers and sisters. When one of my oldest friends had her fourth child and I sat with her and her beautiful new baby at lunch, I couldn't tolerate the jealousy. I had to tell her that I couldn't see her anymore. Living in Jerusalem made my longing even more intense. I was always surrounded by families with so many children, and the mothers were inevitably pregnant.

Sometimes I felt that nothing was left of me except my prayers for getting married and having a child. I cried my prayers. I danced my prayers. I literally got on my knees and begged God. One of my favorite prayer dances was to Bob Dylan's song "Knockin' on Heaven's Door." I was knocking with all my being on heaven's door. When Rosh Hashanah came around year after year, and I was still single and childless, I cried and prayed and begged God to remember me like He remembered Sarah and Hannah, whose stories we read on Rosh Hashanah. One time, while teaching a group of religious women who were all married, I said to them: "All I do is pray to get married. I sometimes wonder what married people pray for." One of the women quickly answered: "We pray because we are married!"

Whether I was right or wrong, it looked to me like the fertile women who surrounded me, who seemed to be easily giving birth to so many sons and daughters, were not begging God for every child. They were not seeing every pregnancy as the greatest of miracles.

I was not infertile, as far as I knew — I just wasn't in the position to have children. With each passing year, with each heartbreak, my situational barrenness opened my eyes wider and wider to seeing that having a child is a miraculous gift from God. And so it was directly to God that I prayed and begged for a child.

I was 38 when I met my husband, Jonathan. We were blessed quickly with the birth of our gorgeous, treasured daughter, קליה תפארת Kalya Tiferet. I was in a state of ecstatic gratitude to God. I knew, like Sarah, in every cell of my body, that she had come from God. The profound gratitude and joy of the miraculous divine gift of my daughter has never left me.

She is most appropriately named after my loving father, Coleman. She has his generous, kind, joyful heart. The letters kuf lamed in her name are in the word הקלה *(hakalah)* relief. The letters yud heh spell one of the names of God. For me, Kalya always will be the loving heart of my father and my relief from God.

Tiferet is one of the ten divine attributes called sefirot. It has many meanings, including beauty, harmony, splendor, healing. Tiferet is the balanced integration of loving-kindness and discipline. We truly were touched with prophecy when we gave her this name, as tiferet is an accurate description of Kalya. It is our prayer that she will always be blessed with the qualities of tiferet.

"Nothing" was Her Child

We return now to the study of Sarah. We saw that the word akara reveals that Sarah was an uprooter, revealing the divine essence of creation.

Playing with the word אין *(eyn)* in the second half of the verse reveals even more:

> **And Sarai was barren,** אין לה ולד *(eyn la valad)*, **she had no child** (B'reishit 11:30).

אין *(Eyn)* means there isn't. The opposite of eyn is יש *(yesh)*. Yesh means there is. For example, yesh mayim means there is water. Yesh ahava means there is love. Everything God creates is called yesh. Stars, time, people, breath, are all yesh.

Usually "eyn la valad" is read as "she had no child." Since אין can be read as eyn or ayin, we can also read this as "ayin is her child." Ayin means nothing. What can "nothing is her child" possibly mean?

God Creates Yesh Me'ayin

Jewish tradition teaches that there is one Creator who creates יש *(yesh)* everything in existence from אין *(ayin)* nothing.

> **God creates everything yesh me'ayin. Out of His nothingness He makes everything in existence** (Sfat Emet, Shmot תרל"ה ד"ה ברש"י).

Ayin must mean more than our ordinary understanding of nothing as absolute absence. Indeed, ayin is infinitely more than nothing. Ayin is the essence of God, who is referred to as Eyn Sof, There Is No End. There is no naming, describing, grasping, defining, comprehending, or imagining the Eyn Sof. Eyn Sof is the absolutely unknowable essence of God. When we wax poetic about how we cannot describe God, we come closer to truth than when we attempt to describe God.

Maimonides speaks about the impossible task of comprehending the Eyn Sof:

> **Because it is has been made clear that He has no physicality or form, none of the actions of the body are appropriate to Him. Neither connection nor separation, neither place nor measure, neither ascent nor descent, neither right nor left, neither front nor back, neither sitting nor standing. He is not found within time so that He would have a beginning, an end, or age. He does not change, for there is nothing that can cause Him to change. Death is not applicable to Him, nor is life within the context of physical life. Foolishness is not applicable to Him, nor is wisdom in terms of human wisdom. Neither sleep nor waking, neither anger nor laughter, neither joy nor sadness, neither silence nor speech in the human understanding of speech** (Mishnah Torah, Hilchot Yesodei HaTorah, Chapter 1).

Although we cannot name or know what ayin is, we are taught that ayin is the infinite source of all yesh. We might have thought that yesh is more than ayin, just as something is more than nothing. No. Yesh is actually only a contracted manifestation of ayin.

> **It is only through the contraction of His light that yesh comes into being** (Sfat Emet, Rosh Hashanah תרנ"ז ד"ה החיים).

Although it is surprising, it is fitting that we refer to the essence of God as nothing, because there is nothing that we, part of contracted yesh, can say or know of the infinite ayin. The angels themselves are always asking: "Where is the place of His glory?" Their question is rhetorical. They know there is no knowing of God. Often the truest expression of devotion and praise is to be silent, to say nothing.

> **For You silence is praise** (Psalms 65:2).

To say that Judaism believes silence is praise may be puzzling at first if one is familiar with Jews and Jewish practice. Although silence plays a role in praising God, most of the time Jewish people are anything but silent in their prayers. From the moment we awake in the morning until the last moment at night, our days are filled with words of prayer and blessing to God. On some holidays, like Rosh Hashanah and Yom Kippur, we pray all day, saying every word in a prayer book that is hundreds of pages long. Words are so essential in our relationship to God that the Rabbis teach that our greatest power is in our mouth, and that we were created for the sake of praising God.

> **I have created this people for me, they will speak my praises** (Isaiah 43:21).

We see here a contradiction between silent praise and spoken praise. This reflects a bigger contradiction between not knowing God and knowing God. In Proverbs we are instructed:

> **In all of your ways, know Him** (Proverbs 3:6).

How do we resolve this paradox that, on one hand, there is nothing we can know or say about God, and on the other hand, we are created to know God and sing His praises? The resolution lies in understanding that, while the Eyn Sof is utterly concealed and unknowable, we can know what God "shares" with His creation. What He shares is referred to as His glory.

> **Even though the Holy One is concealed and there is absolutely no grasping Him at all, even so, He is capable of all, and He created the world in a way that His glory, which fills all the worlds, is revealed through yesh** (Sfat Emet, Purim תרמ״ט ד״ה בפסוק).

We are meant to say and know a lot about God's glory in His creation. But however elevated our words and consciousness becomes, the bridge between the Eyn Sof and His creation can never be crossed in the mind, imagination, or experience. The more we praise God for what He makes knowable of Himself in creation, the more we realize how unknowable and ineffable His essence is.

I HAD A GLIMPSE OF the divine unknowable when I was 19 years old and went snorkeling in the Red Sea. I was enjoying all the colorful fish around the coral reef when suddenly I came to the drop-off, the place at the end of the reef that opens into a breathtaking expanse of water. Coming from Minnesota, where we had lakes but no ocean, I had never seen anything so profoundly vast and deep before. It was good that I was holding the hand of a confident Israeli man, because I was overwhelmed. It literally took my breath away. I felt minuscule in the face of that vast expanse.

I realized then that being in relationship with God is like being a fish in the ocean. The deeper into the vast ocean we go, the more we become aware of how small we are. The deeper we dive into knowing God in His creation, the more we realize His vast unknowable essence. Turning our gaze toward the Eyn Sof is like swimming into a divine drop-off. All that is left is silence and awe.

With our expanding definitions of עקרה *(akara)* and אין *(eyn, ayin)*, the usual translation of "Sarah was barren, she had no child" transforms to:

Sarah was the uprooter of ordinary consciousness, who gave birth to the awareness that God is the ineffable, unknowable, infinite source of all that is.

The Task of Returning Yesh to Ayin

Chassidic wisdom is full of teachings about God creating the world yesh me'ayin something from nothing, and about the purpose of creation, which is to connect all yesh back to its source in ayin.

> **The purpose of creation is that yesh should surrender itself into the realm of ayin** (Sfat Emet, Rosh Hashanah תרנ"ז ד"ה החיים).

> **The עיקר *(ikar)* essential intention of a person in his prayers and his Torah should be to direct himself always to the עיקר *(ikar)* essence of all, the One who gives existence to all, the elevated Eyn Sof** (Reishit Chochmah, Gateway of Holiness, Chapter 12).

Although we cannot know the Eyn Sof, we are meant to direct our thoughts, speech, and action toward it always. By connecting our world, yesh to ayin, we bring more divinity into our world. We bring ayin into yesh. In other words, we reveal God in His creation.

In the words of Rebbe Abraham Friedman HaMalach:

> **God created yesh from ayin in order that the righteous ones will make ayin out of yesh. What this means is that God created everything in existence from the starting point of ayin. It was clothed and contracted from level to level until it became physical yesh. The righteous ones, out of their awe of God, surrender all physical reality to God. By doing this, they draw down the divine into the lowest levels** (Chesed L'Avraham).

Reality is always filled with God, whether we see it or not, whether we attach to it or not. If it was not connected to God, it would not exist. It is just that the connection of reality to the Creator is hidden. Connecting yesh back to its source in ayin reveals God's presence in creation.

> It is brought in the Gemara that the actions of the righteous ones are greater than the creation of heaven and earth. The creation of heaven and earth was yesh me'ayin, and the righteous ones make ayin from yesh, because in everything that they do, even physical things like eating, they raise up the holy sparks (Maggid of Mezritch, Maggid D'varav L'Yaakov).

What a wild idea! For human beings to act in a way that reveals God's presence is even greater than God's creation of heaven and earth.

By giving birth to ayin, Sarah birthed the path of reconnecting yesh to ayin, of revealing God's life-giving presence. It is the work of her children to continue the task. By revealing God's presence, we raise up holy sparks and increase light.

> It is God's will that the Children of Israel increase light through their good actions (Sfat Emet, Titzaveh תרל״א ד״ה במדרש).

How in the world do we do this? The Torah gives directions. Those directions are called mitzvahs.

> The Children of Israel need to return the yesh of creation back to its source in ayin, by connecting all of life to Torah and by performing mitzvahs (Sfat Emet, Rosh Hashanah תרמ״ב ד״ה עשרת).

7
Connecting to Holiness

What are מצוות *(mitzvot)* mitzvahs and how do they connect yesh back to ayin? Not surprisingly, there are many answers to this question.

Mitzvahs Are Connectors

The most common understanding of mitzvah is commandment. There are 613 mitzvahs in the Torah, covering all aspects of human behavior from thought to speech to action. They are divided into 248 mitzvahs of action, and 365 mitzvahs of refraining from action. Studying Torah, lighting Shabbat candles, hearing the sound of the shofar, are mitzvahs of action. Not stealing, not lighting a fire on Shabbat, not eating leavened bread on Passover are mitzvahs of refraining from action.

The sages linked the word מצוה *(mitzvah)* with the word צותא *(tzavtah)* connection.

Mitzvah means connection (Kedushat Levi, Vayera).

What a surprising and radically different understanding — to see mitzvahs not only as commandments, but as connectors! What do mitzvahs connect?

Mitzvahs connect body to soul, earth to heaven, external to internal, this world to the world to come, man to God, yesh to ayin. Mitzvahs are God's directions for connecting the creation to the Creator.

Through mitzvahs the Children of Israel connect to God (Sfat Emet, Titzaveh תרל"א ד"ה במדרש).

Candles and Light

Torah and mitzvahs are compared to light and a candle.

A mitzvah is a candle and Torah is light (Proverbs 6:23).

Torah is called light. It is the concealed light of God.

The light of Torah is above the comprehension of human beings (Sfat Emet, Titzaveh תרמ"ג ד"ה בפסוק).

Sfat Emet repeatedly reminds us that Torah:

... is concealed from the eyes of all living things (Job 28:21).

The incomprehensible, concealed light of Torah has the power to illuminate all creation. Torah needs a candle to burn to make its divine light visible. Mitzvahs are that candle.

The Torah is light, but we cannot draw close to the light of Torah except through the candle of mitzvah, through which the Children of Israel become vessels for receiving the light of Torah (Sfat Emet, Succoth תרס"ב ד"ה נגיל).

Torah Dressed as Action

Mitzvahs are the light of Torah, dressed up as physical actions that illuminate the spiritual darkness of the world (Sfat Emet, VaYishlach תרמ"ח ד"ה עם).

This is an exceptionally elevated way to see mitzvahs, but it is not a common understanding. Mitzvahs are sometimes dismissed as meaningless or outdated religious actions or restrictions. Even for many mitzvah-observing people, it is not obvious that doing a mitzvah reveals the light of Torah. But Torah and mitzvahs are not coming to teach us about the obvious. They connect us to the secret divine illumination embedded in everything.

One of my favorite examples of misunderstanding mitzvahs as meaningless action was the time a friend, bewildered by my traditional observance of eating only kosher food, asked my mother:

"Why does Diane think there is anything spiritual about eating? Food is just food!"

Food is Not Just Food

We see in the blessing after eating bread that there is something very spiritual about eating, and that food is not just food. The blessing begins:

> **Blessed are You, our God, King of the world, who nourishes the whole world with His goodness, with grace, with love, and compassion.**

It continues:

> **He gives bread to all flesh, because His love is forever** (Birkat HaMazon).

Before even mentioning bread, this blessing describes being nourished with goodness, grace, love, and compassion. Food, like everything in creation, is made of physical and spiritual ingredients.

On the verse:

> **Man does not live by bread alone but by all that comes out of the mouth of God** (D'varim 8:3).

Sfat Emet teaches:

> **All food is combined with illumination that comes from the mouth of God that is inextricably woven into the bread** (Sfat Emet, B'shalach תרמ"ז ד"ה בענין).

God's light is kneaded into our food. When we eat, we are meant to taste and be nourished not only by the physical, but by the spiritual, by the divine light and goodness in the food.

> **A righteous person eats to satisfy his soul** (Proverbs 13:25).

There are many mitzvahs that instruct us what to eat and not eat, when to eat and not eat, why to eat and not eat, where to eat and not eat. These mitzvahs awaken the taste buds of our soul, so we can taste and see God's satisfying spiritual ingredients in our food.

Taste and see that God is good (Psalm 34:8).

Mitzvahs Add Life to Life

The essence of one's vitality comes from being occupied with Torah and mitzvahs. The more a person invests his energy in mitzvahs, the more new life he is given. And not only more vitality, but life at a higher level. There are many levels to life, and a person must always elevate himself from one level to the next. This is what is meant by "to walk in the ways of Torah, and to live by them" (Sfat Emet, Acharei Mot תרמ"ד ד"ה בפסוק).

Life and death are not absolute states. One is neither simply alive or dead. One can be in various states of life or death while alive, and even after death.

The Talmud says:

The evil are called dead even when they are physically alive, and the righteous are called alive even after they have died (Babylonian Talmud, Brachot 18a).

The Torah is called the Tree of Life. The more we attach to the Tree of Life, the more alive we become.

When you do a mitzvah, it is as if you are lighting a candle before the Holy One, and you bring life to your soul (Midrash Rabbah, Shmot 36:3).

Going back to eating, we see that eating is not only for the sake of keeping us alive, or even for the great pleasure we receive. In the context of mitzvahs, a meal is elevated into being an enlivening, candle-lit feast for the soul.

So, in answer to my friend's question, food is not just food; there is something very spiritual in eating.

Soul and Body

Torah and mitzvahs are like soul and body. Torah is the soul; mitzvahs are the body.

> **Doing mitzvahs, a person draws the light of Torah into the mitzvahs. This is how the soul illuminates the body** (Sfat Emet, B'Ha'alotcha תרמ״ז-תרמ״ח-תרנ״ב ד״ה במדרש).

God gave us our souls when He created us.

> **And He blew into his nostrils** נשמת חיים *(nishmat chayyim)* **the soul of life and the human being became a living soul** (B'reishit 2:7).

Sfat Emet elaborates:

> **The Holy One attached our soul to our body. The soul is embedded in the body like a wellspring under the earth. Just as one must dig a well to find water, a person must put forth effort to find his soul within him** (Sfat Emet, Toldot תרנ״ז ד״ה בענין).

Even though God attached our soul to our body, it takes effort to discover it. Mitzvahs are the tools for discovering the living waters of our soul.

The Zohar teaches that the 613 mitzvahs correspond to the structure of the human body.

> A person's 248 limbs correspond to the 248 mitzvahs of action in the Torah. These mitzvahs are 248 angelic forces that bring God's presence into creation. The 365 sinews in the body correspond to the 365 mitzvahs of refraining from action (Zohar 1:170b).

We cannot illuminate creation with the light of Torah without mitzvahs. So too

> We cannot comprehend our souls except through the actions of the body, the body that corresponds to the 613 mitzvahs (Sfat Emet, B'Ha'alotcha תרמ"א ד"ה במדרש).

> The human being is created in the image of God. This image is revealed through the 248 mitzvahs of action, and the 365 mitzvahs of refraining from action (Sfat Emet, תר"נ ד"ה וביום).

Illuminating our souls through the body of mitzvahs, we reveal what it means to be created in the image of God.

Illuminating the Body of the World

The human being is a microcosm of the entire world — עולם קטן (olam katan) a small world.

> The design of the world corresponds to the 613 limbs and sinews of the human being (Sfat Emet, VaYishlach תרל"א ד"ה ויחן).

When we illuminate ourselves with mitzvahs, we illuminate the corresponding parts of the world as well.

The Matok MiDvash commentary on the Zohar laments that:

> **We do not know which part of creation corresponds to which limbs of a human being. The ancient ones knew this wisdom, but it has been lost** (Matok MiDvash, Zohar 1:134b).

Even though the details of the correspondence between mitzvahs, limbs, and the world are lost, how awesome to consider that:

> **Man is the intermediary between Torah and the world, and by being occupied with Torah we bring abundant blessing to all of creation** (Matok MiDvash, Zohar 1:134:b).

Weaving Garments of Light

Doing mitzvahs, we illuminate the body and the world with the light of Torah.

In the beginning, when we were in the Garden of Eden, we were clothed in garments of light.

> **At first Adam and Eve were dressed in the elevated light of the Garden of Eden. If they hadn't been clothed in that light, they could not have entered there. When they were expelled, they needed a different garment. Therefore, it is written that God clothed them in a garment of skin. Every soul is dressed according to its needs, according to the time, the place, and its merit** (Zohar 2:229b).

The Hebrew words אור *(or)* light and עור *(or)* skin sound the same but are spelled differently. Light begins with א *(aleph)*, which has the gematria of one and hints to God's oneness. Skin begins with ע *(ayin)*, which has the gematria of seventy and hints to the great diversity of the world, where God's oneness is hidden. God's oneness is a secret hidden in the world. That is why the word סוד *(sod)* secret is also seventy. Being clothed in garments of light was appropriate in the place of revealed, divine light. Once expelled from the garden, we needed different garments.

> **And the Lord God made garments of skin for Adam and his wife, and He clothed them** (B'reishit 3:21).

These garments of skin are our physical bodies. Our physical bodies are the appropriate clothing for life outside the garden.

HAVING GROWN UP IN MINNESOTA, I know the importance of wearing the right garment for the right weather. To go outside in the way below zero winter temperatures, we dress in many layers of very warm clothing. Without these warm garments we would not last long in the bitter cold.

To live in the physical world outside the Garden of Eden, we need the right garments. But we are not meant to live in only a physical world. We are meant to live in a physical-spiritual world. To live in a physical-spiritual world, we need the appropriate garments. Our work is to transform our physical bodies so we can live in a world illuminated by the light of Torah. The light revealed by doing mitzvahs transforms the physical into the physical-spiritual. Sfat Emet calls this physical-spiritual body a garment for the soul.

> **A person acquires garments for his soul through his actions** (Sfat Emet, Toldot תרמ"ז ד"ה בפסוק).

In the Garden of Eden, God gave us garments of light. Outside the garden, we weave our own garments, integrating our עור *(or)* skin-bodies with the אור *(or)* of Torah. With our mitzvah-woven garments, we live an ever-brighter life.

A Spiritual Scent

We cannot see when our physical body has become a physical-spiritual garment. Our bodies look the same — but they have a spiritual scent that we can become aware of. This is like the scent of food from the kitchen that wafts through the house that we can smell without ever seeing the actual food.

> We can't reveal things of the next world in this world, but we can smell the scent of these higher worlds in this world (Sfat Emet, Toldot תרמ"ז ד"ה בפסוק).

There is a beautiful story in the Zohar about the scent of mitzvah-woven garments:

> Two important guests, Rabbi Yitzchak and Rabbi Yehuda, come to the home of the late Rabbi Hamnuna Saba. Rabbi Hamnuna's widow tells her young son, already known for his great spiritual sensitivity, to go to these wise men to receive a blessing. The young boy begins to approach the visiting Rabbis, but turns back. He says to his mother, "I don't want to come close to them, because they did not say 'Hear, O Israel, the Lord our God, the Lord is One' today in its right time." When asked how he knew that, the boy answered, "When I got close to them, I knew from the scent of their garments" (Zohar 3:186a).

There are 248 words in the traditional recitation of the daily Shma, Hear, O Israel prayer (Shulchan Aruch, Orach Chayyim 61:3). These words correspond to the 248 limbs of the human body, and the 248 mitzvahs of action. The mitzvah of reciting this prayer weaves a scented garment for the soul, sewn letter by letter, limb by limb, mitzvah by mitzvah.

This young boy had spiritual sensitivity so refined that he was aware of the lack of the scent of this prayer in their garments.

Having learned a few things now about Hebrew, Torah, Sarah, Avraham, and mitzvahs, it is time to consider an essential aspect of all of these realms: קדושה *(kedusha)* holiness.

Holiness

What is holiness? To define holiness is similar to trying to define Torah and Hebrew. All these realms that emanate from the ever-unknowable God cannot be easily defined. In the book ראשית חכמה *(Reishit Chochmah)* The Beginning of Wisdom, Rabbi Eliyahu De Vidas wrote over four hundred pages on holiness. His teachings are a drop in the Torah ocean of wisdom on the subject. Once again, I invite you to knock on heaven's door with me and ask for the gift of a glimpse of the meaning of holiness. We begin with God and the Jewish people.

One definition of קדושה *(kedusha)* holiness is set apart. God is קדוש *(kadosh)* holy.

I, the Lord your God, am holy (VaYikra 19:2).

God is called הקדוש ברוך הוא *(HaKadosh Baruch Hu)* The Holy One, blessed be He. The Holy One is the ultimate set apart One. The greatest Torah sages have always contemplated and written about the utter separateness of the Holy One from His creation.

Because holiness is referring to a Godly realm that is wholly set apart from creation, we might think that holiness is exclusive to God and therefore inaccessible within creation. And yet the Torah tells us, over and over, that not only is God holy, but we too are meant to be holy.

> **Speak to the whole community of the Children of Israel and say to them: Be holy because I, the Lord your God, am holy** (VaYikra 19:2).
>
> **And make yourselves holy, and you will be holy, because I am the Lord your God** (VaYikra 20:7).
>
> **And you will be a holy people for me** (Shmot 22:30).

Even though holiness refers to a separate Godly realm:

> **Every person has the potential to become holy in all his actions, even though he is within the natural world** (Sfat Emet, Kedoshim תרל"א ד"ה קדושים).

Mitzvahs Are Signposts to Holiness

Sfat Emet asks:

> **How can flesh and blood become holy?** (Sfat Emet, Kedoshim תרל"א ד"ה קדושים)

In one of his many answers to this question, he says:

> **A person must occupy himself in Torah and mitzvahs in order to draw holiness into the body** (Sfat Emet, Kedoshim תרס"ג ד"ה עוד).

The beginning of the blessing we say before doing a mitzvah reveals the connection between mitzvahs and becoming holy:

> **Blessed are You, Lord, our God, King of the Universe, who made us holy through His mitzvahs and commanded us to...**

After saying this opening phrase, we complete the blessing by specifying which mitzvah we are doing. For example, light the Shabbat candles, occupy ourselves in Torah study, eat matzah, sit in a succah, wave the lulav, and all other mitzvahs of action.

Amazingly enough, even though we say this before doing all our mitzvahs, most of us are surprised to discover the great secret it reveals in simple language: God makes us holy through His mitzvahs.

The word מצוה (*mitzvah*) shares letters with the word ציון (*tzi'oon*) signpost. Mitzvahs are signposts pointing us in the direction of holiness.

> **All the mitzvahs, even though they are physical actions, are like signposts from the Holy One in the Torah. Through the mitzvah-signpost, we can attach to the holiness within it, which is the Torah. In truth, mitzvahs are the wisdom of how to draw down His holiness into all our actions** (Sfat Emet, Kedoshim תרל״ב ד״ה במדרש).

> **Mitzvahs are physical actions that are hints and signposts to elevated worlds. By doing the mitzvahs, we merit the holiness of Torah** (Sfat Emet, Kedoshim תרל״ו ד״ה במדרש).

God is Hiding in the Word Mitzvah

Playing with atbash, we discover God's name in the word מצוה (*mitzvah*). מ (*Mem*) is the tenth letter from the end of the alephbet, and י (*yud*) is the tenth letter from the beginning. צ (*Tzadi*) is the fifth letter from the end of the alephbet, and ה (*heh*) is the fifth from the beginning. So, with atbash, mem-tzadi transforms into yud-heh and the word מצוה *(mitzvah)* is revealed as י-ה-ו-ה *(yud-heh-vav-heh)*, the four-letter name of God.

Every mitzvah has a hidden and revealed aspect to it. The י-ה *(yud-heh)* is the hidden aspect of mitzvahs. That is why yud-heh is hidden in mem-tzadi. The ו-ה *(vav-heh)* is the revealed aspect of mitzvah.

> **The hidden aspect of the mitzvah hints to the realm of ayin. That is why the letters yud-heh are hidden, because ayin is hidden. The letters vav-heh are the revealed aspect of the mitzvah, and refer to the world of yesh** (Kedushat Levi, B'reishit 1).

The letters of the word mitzvah reveal the secret of mitzvahs. Doing mitzvahs, we connect what's revealed-yesh, to what's hidden-ayin. Connecting yesh to ayin, we reveal God's name-yud-heh-vav-heh. Revealing God's name, we draw holiness into creation.

Separation for the Sake of Connecting

Rabbi Eliyahu de Vidas expands our understanding by teaching that there are two aspects of holiness.

> **One is the aspect of separation. The second is the drawing of the light of holiness into our lives** (Reishit Chochmah, Gate of Holiness, Chapter 1).

The first aspect of becoming holy comes from separating ourselves from certain parts of the world that are the opposite of holiness.

> **God is holy and spiritual, and you are physical. The spiritual can only dwell in the physical through holiness, which is separation** (Reishit Chochmah, Gate of Holiness, Chapter 1).

There are 365 mitzvahs of refraining from action. They separate us from certain parts of creation in order to be holy.

The second aspect of holiness is drawing down the light of holiness. The holiness of God is like the sun that is always shining. It is waiting to be drawn into the world. We separate from the unholy in order to open the curtains and draw the light of holiness into our lives. We separate from the unholy for the sake of connecting to God.

> **Be holy so that you can connect to your God, and so that God will dwell within you** (Reishit Chochmah, Gate of Holiness, Chapter 1).

While it is true that an aspect of holiness comes from separating from the world, the Torah does not prescribe a completely ascetic life, removed from society and the pleasures of the world. Together with the 365 mitzvahs of refraining, we have 248 mitzvahs of action that teach us how to live in creation. Altogether, the 613 mitzvahs of doing and refraining are the way to both separate from and live within the world in order to be holy.

God could have made this world holy from the start — but he left it up to us. He wanted us to have the great merit of transforming a physical world with no apparent holiness into a holy place. The task of revealing holiness in the world is given to the Jewish people.

> **The Holy One, who can do everything, could have created this world with a revealed holiness, like in the upper worlds. But He made this lower world physical, and without a revelation of holiness. It is through performance of the mitzvahs of the Jewish people that holiness is revealed** (Sfat Emet, Titzaveh תרנ"א ד"ה ובמדרש).

Holiness and Chol

That which is not holy, but is permitted, is called חול *(chol)*. Chol is not in the realm of the holy but has the potential to be.

Parchment and ink are chol. But when you write a sefer Torah, the parchment and ink become holy. Flour and water mixed together are chol. But when you eat it as matzah at the Passover seder, the eating becomes holy.

This is in distinction to that which is forbidden and can never become holy. A sefer Torah written on nonkosher parchment can never become holy. Eating bread on Passover is not holy, and does not have the potential to become holy.

There are three realms when thinking about holiness: The holy, the unholy that we must separate from, and the chol, that which is not yet holy or unholy and has potential to go either way. Our thought, speech, and actions can exist in any of these three realms.

חול *(Chol)* is related to חלל *(chalal)* empty space. Chol is everything in creation that is empty of holiness, but is waiting to be filled with it.

Rav Kook teaches that holiness is built on the foundation of the chol. The chol is the material for the holy. Holiness needs chol within which it can manifest its great light.

> **First chol awakens, and afterwards it is imperative that the holy will awaken, to complete the chol** (Maamarei Ha'RaAya, Collection of Rav Kook's Writings, Part 2).

The letters of חול *(chol)* are in the word מחול *(machol)* dance. If we think of chol as the body of the world and holy as the soul that animates the body and moves it into holiness, we can say that holiness and chol are two elements in the dance of creation. Without a body, the holy cannot dance. Without the holy, there is no dance.

8
Heavenly Names – Secrets of the Yud

Our Name and Our Soul

We have seen that Sarah gave birth to ayin, connecting the created world to holiness, yesh to ayin. Giving birth to ayin, Sarah births the divine dance of holiness and chol.

We are ready now to dive into Sarah's name. Names are enormously significant in Torah and Jewish tradition. A person's name contains his purpose in life and the essence of his soul.

Rabbi Akiva Tatz says שם *(shem)*

> "... also means a 'name,' always a definition of essence in Torah; and it means 'there' in the sense of a destination or end-point, the essence, the purpose, of any journey or process. This is also the root of the word for the ultimate destination, *shamayim*, 'heaven,' in the sense of life's destination; the word *shamayim* literally spells out the plural of destination, *'shamim'*, that is, the composite of all 'theres' that are possible, the culmination of all journeys, the final essence" (*Letters to a Buddhist Jew*, page 79).

Naming a Jewish child is an awesome responsibility and task. The Rabbis teach that parents are given a touch of prophecy when naming a child.

> When a child is born and his father and mother give him a name that comes to them, it is not random. It is the Holy One that puts the name that is essential for that soul in their mouths (Rabbi Yitzchak Luria, Shaar HaGilgulim).

How else would parents be wise enough to know the essence of their child's soul and purpose in life if not for being touched with prophecy and receiving the name from God?

For Sfat Emet, name and soul are almost inter-changeable concepts.

> Every person's soul is made up of unique letters. And that is the name he was created for (Sfat Emet, Shmot תרנ"ז ד"ה ואלה).

Playing with the letters ש-ם *(shin-mem)* Rabbi Akiva Tatz points out that שם *(shem)* name is part of the word נשמה *(neshama)* soul. Our שם *(shem)* name resides שם *(sham)* there in our נשמה *(neshama)* soul.

God engraves the Hebrew letters of our soul-filled names within us.

> The letters that the Holy One engraves within us must become clear to us in all ways, until we bring the potential in our names, our souls, our unique letters, into actuality (Sfat Emet, Shmot תרנ"ז ד"ה ואלה).

Like the DNA of a tree that is encoded with genetic instructions for its development, our names are our spiritual DNA, encoded with divine wisdom for our development. When the seed of a tree first sprouts, the tree reveals the tiniest green shoot. As the years go on the tree's powerful trunk, vibrant green leaves, and sweet fruit reveal more and more of the potential encoded in its DNA.

We must clarify and manifest the potential in our names. Then we will grow, like a tree, reaching up to touch higher worlds, reaching up to touch heaven.

Our Name and God's Name

In the daily prayer the Kaddish, we acknowledge that God's name grows.

> **Yitgadal veyitkadash Shmei rabbah means God's great name will grow greater and become more holy** (Kaddish prayer).

God gave us the name Israel. God includes His name, אל *(El)*, in our name, ישראל *(Yisrael)* Israel. This is what we are referring to when we say:

> **You called us by Your name** (Ein Kitzva prayer, Musaf on Rosh Hashanah).

The letters in ישראל *(Yisrael)* Israel can be divided into two words, ישר *(yashar)* straight and אל *(El)* God. By rearranging the letters we also discover שיר *(shir)* song and אל *(El)* God. Our name expresses our purpose: to be aligned with God and sing His praises.

Because our name is connected to God's name, by manifesting our purpose as individuals and unifying as a people we reveal more of the ever-growing, holy name of God.

> **To the extent that the Children of Israel unify, the glory of God's name grows greater** (Sfat Emet, Purim תרל"ד ד"ה מה).

Not only does God's name grow, but our awareness of God's name grows. By growing our awareness of God's holy name, we reveal more of the Tree of Life, more of God's presence in the world.

Clarifying Our Names Through Exile

Exile is one way to clarify and manifest the purpose encoded in our names. Sfat Emet learns this from the first verse of שמות *(Shmot)*. Although Shmot is called Exodus in English, it literally means Names.

And these are the names of the Children of Israel (Shmot 1:1).

The names of the Children of Israel were already listed toward the end of the book of B'reishit. Why are they listed again in Shmot? The Midrash teaches that the word "and" in this verse indicates that what is being told now adds to what has come before. Sfat Emet understands that the Torah repeats the names of the Children of Israel when they descend into Egypt to teach that their names grew and clarified in exile.

Through exile their names grew greatly and became clarified and more whole (Sfat Emet, Shmot ואלה ד"ה תרנ"ז).

What is exile and how does it help us clarify our names? On one level, exile refers to the Jewish people being outside of the Land of Israel.

On another level, Rav Kook teaches that

exile is disconnection from our essential selves — and therefore from God (Orot HaKodesh, Volume 3).

Because exile is disconnection from our essence, we can also say it is disconnection from our names.

Exile is not comfortable. There is an existential angst in being disconnected from our place, our self, and God. It is this discomfort of disconnection, of not knowing who we essentially are, of not knowing our names, that motivates us to search out and find our names. Paradoxically, exile is a catalyst for knowing our names and growing full spiritual lives.

Exile as Boon

Author Clarissa Pinkola Estes describes the spiritual advantages of exile based on the fairy tale of the ugly duckling:

> "If you have attempted to fit whatever mold and failed to do so, you are probably lucky. You may be an exile of some sort, but you have sheltered your soul.... There is something useful in all this torque and tension. Something in the duckling is being tempered, being made strong by this exile. While this situation is not one we would wish on anyone for any reason, its effect is similar to pure natural carbon under pressure producing diamonds — it leads eventually to a profound magnitude and clarity of psyche.... Even though there are negative aspects to it, the wild psyche can endure exile. It makes us yearn that much more to free our own true nature and causes us to long for a culture that goes with it" (*Women Who Run with the Wolves*, page 186).

Sfat Emet reveals some of the secrets of גלות (*galut*) exile hiding in the Hebrew letters:

> Through exile, the powers of the soul go through transformational growth in many ways, therefore the root of the word גלות (*galut*) exile is the same as the root of the word התגלות (*hitgalut*) inner revelation, like a גל (*gal*) wave and a גלגל (*galgal*) wheel that turn a person around through trials and exiles until he brings forth from potential into actuality all the illumination of his body and soul (Sfat Emet, Shmot תרנ"ז ד"ה ואלה).

The trials of exile are transformational experiences that can reveal the meaning of our names, the purpose of our souls.

Our Name is Our Book

The gematria of שם *(shem)* name is the same as the gematria of ספר *(sefer)* book: ש *(shin)* 300 plus ם *(mem)* 40, and ס *(samech)* 60 plus פ *(peh)* 80 plus ר *(resh)* 200 — both add up to 340. Living our lives, we are always writing the longhand version of our names. My life is my book. Every person's life is a unique book that needs to be written.

Torah is the book of God's name.

> The whole Torah is the Holy Name of God. There is not one word in the Torah that is not part of the Holy Name (Zohar 2:87b).

In the novel *The Lord of the Rings*, author J.R.R. Tolkien writes about the great significance of names. When the Hobbit named Merry hears the Tree person calling himself an Ent, he asks:

> "An Ent?" said Merry. "What's that? But what do you call yourself? What's your real name?"

The Ent replies:

> "Hoo now!" replied Treebeard. "Hoo! Now that would be telling! Not so hasty."

Further on in the same conversation about names, the Ent says:

> "'Hm, but you are hasty folk, I see,' said Treebeard. 'I am honored by your confidence; but you should not be too free all at once…. For I am not going to tell you my name, not yet at any rate….' 'For one thing it would take a long while: my name is growing all the time, and I've lived a very long, long time; so *my* name is like a story. Real names tell you the story of the things they belong to in my language, in the Old Entish as you might say. It is a lovely language, but it

takes a very long time to say anything in it, because we do not say anything in it, unless it is worth taking a long time to say, and to listen to" (*The Lord of the Rings*, pages 453-454).

Knowing that names are prophetic expressions of essence and purpose, realizing that names are books, we begin now to dive into the book of Sarah's name. If you want to know what Sarah's name really is, I need a very long time to talk. And you need a very long time to listen.

Sarai שרי - The Master of the Yud

In the beginning, Sarah is called שרי (*Sarai*). Dividing Sarai's name into two parts gives שר (*sar*) and י (*yud*). שר (*Sar*) means master. Sarai was the spiritual master of the yud.

What is yud?

Harry Potter and the Hebrew Letters

Studying the secrets of the Hebrew letters reminds me of a story from Harry Potter. Harry is told that to get to his school of magic he has to go to platform 9 ¾ at the train station. The problem is that he sees platforms 9 and 10, but he can't find platform 9 ¾. Harry needs help and encouragement from those who have gone before him. To find platform 9 ¾ he must run right into a solid wall. Running straight into the wall, Harry discovers that it isn't as it seems. He magically passes through.

Like Harry Potter at the train station, if one has not yet been a student in the school of Hebrew letters, one may approach the letters and not see any opening. But the masters of the Hebrew letters assure us that there are openings. Just as Harry needed guidance to find an opening that was not visible, so too students who want to penetrate into the Hebrew letters must be guided by a teacher.

Our sages have been guiding students into the secrets of the Hebrew letters for thousands of years. Studying Hebrew letters, there is much to consider.

Rabbi Yaakov Koppel teaches that every letter has three aspects: its name, its shape, and its gematria. (Shaarai Gan Eden, Shaar Ha Otiot, Ot aleph). Seeking knowledge of the secrets of Hebrew letters is a rare pursuit. With humility, we now dive into the letter yud.

The Raw Material of all Letters

Rabbi Abraham ben David, the Raavad, said:

> **The letter yud is unformed raw material** (Raavad, Sefer Yetzirah 1:1).

When yud is written out by a Torah scribe, it has a form.

But the essence of the yud is actually only the first point of contact of the inked quill with the parchment. It is almost imperceptible. This dimensionless point is the beginning point of all letters.

In truth, all letters are a series of connected yud points.

> **The yud is the beginning point of all the letters. And the end point. And it is hidden within them. And it is impossible for any of the holy letters to exist without the yud** (Raavad, Sefer Yetzirah 1:1).

The three letters that spell out the name of the letter yud are י *(yud)*, ו *(vav)*, and ד *(dalet)*. These letters depict how yud moves from its dimensionless, formless point into dimensional forms.

> **The first letter of the word yud is the non-dimensional point. When drawn down vertically, the י *yud* becomes a line, which is the ו (*vav*), a one-dimensional form. When a second line is drawn out horizontally, the ו (*vav*) becomes a ד (*dalet*), a two-dimensional form. The yud is extended to become all the lines of all the letters** (Isaiah Horowitz, Shnei Luchot HaBrit, Toldot Adam).

Rearranging the order of the letters that spell out yud, we get דיו *(di'yo)* ink. Ink is like yud — it is unformed raw material for writing letters. If we had purely spiritual eyes, we would see in a jar of black ink the spiritual yud, vibrant with infinite potential to manifest as the letters and words of Torah.

The Transitional Point between the Infinite and the Finite

God is unknowable. There is no form, no letter, no name that can fully reveal God. All forms, letters, and names for God are a constriction of His ultimate essence.

> **The Creator cannot be captured by any letter, vowel, or tiny point** (Kedushat Levi, Rosh Hashanah).

God creates the world with words that are made up of letters that are all essentially the letter yud. Yud is the portal between the quill of the Infinite Creator and the parchment of His creation. God, whose essence is beyond expression, creates the world with the letter yud, the imperceptible point of transition between formlessness and form. Yud is the infinite potential for creation.

Higher Wisdom and Yud

The Hebrew word חכמה *(chochmah)* is used by the sages to refer to two different kinds of wisdom. Sometimes it refers to human wisdom. More often it refers to divine wisdom. In the mystical tradition, divine wisdom is called חכמה עלאה *(chochmah ila'a)* higher wisdom.

The Raavad teaches that, like yud, chochmah is also unformed raw material. He equates higher wisdom with yud.

> **The letter yud, which is unformed raw material, is** חכמה **(*chochmah*), higher wisdom** (Raavad, Sefer Yetzirah 1:1).

The Zohar says:

> **Higher wisdom is called yud** (Zohar 3:243a).

With gematria we see the connection between raw material and higher wisdom.

> **The gematria of גל״ם** *(golem)* **raw material is 73. This is the same as the gematria for חכמה** *(chochmah)* (Raavad, Sefer Yetzirah 1:1).

God makes everything in creation with the raw material of higher wisdom. We acknowledge this every morning in our prayers.

> **You made everything with chochmah** (Morning Prayers).

> **Rearranging the letters of חכמה** *(chochmah)*, **we find כח** *(koach)* **and מה** *(mah)*. **Koach is potential and power. Mah means what, and refers to all that is. Chochmah is the potential that powers all that is** (Zohar 3:235b).

> **Higher wisdom is the beginning point of all that exists. And the end point of all. And it is in everything and concealed from everything. And it is impossible that anything would exist without it** (Raavad, Sefer Yetzirah 1:1).

Rabbi Yaakov Koppel summarizes the yud–higher wisdom connection:

> **The letter yud is called raw material. It is a hint to higher wisdom. Just like raw material has no form, and receives all forms, and all forms are created from it, so too the letter yud has no form. And you cannot write any form of a letter if you do not first start with a point. Yud is the reishit, the beginning point, for the forms of the letters. Higher wisdom is just like this. It is the hidden part of thought that does not yet have any form, and it is the beginning point of all forms** (Shaarei Gan Eden, Shaar HaOtiot, Ot Yud).

Because all letters begin with yud, Rabbi Yaakov Koppel calls the yud ראשית (reishit) first.

Higher wisdom is also reishit (Sefer HaBahir 3).

As we have seen, Torah is also reishit.

Weaving this into the first verse of the Torah, we now understand:

ב *(b)* With

ראשית *(reishit)*

With yud – higher wisdom, God created the heavens and the earth.

One Dressed as Ten

Yud is the tenth letter of the alephbet. The Maharal of Prague teaches that yud hints to God's oneness within our world.

The letter yud is ten, yet yud is an indivisible small point. It indicates that ten are organized together as one (Netivot Olam, Netiv HaTorah, Chapter 1).

Nurit G'al Dor elaborates on the paradox of ten being one:

On one hand, yud represents multiplicity, because its value is ten. On the other hand, it is a single unified entity which cannot be divided (Zera Avraham Ohavi, page 24).

How brilliant that the indivisible One uses an indivisible point, made up of ten, to create the world. Yud whispers the secret that God's oneness creates and underlies His endlessly diverse world.

On this subject Sfat Emet says:

How can many come out of the singular Oneness? The answer is: because God can do anything (Sfat Emet, BaMidbar תרל"ו ד"ה במדרש).

This answer may seem radically unsatisfying, but I see this as an expression of Sfat Emet's humility. He knows that God's ways are ultimately impenetrable mysteries beyond the realm of complete human comprehension.

Only God knows how to create a world that manifests in great diversity out of His absolute, indivisible Oneness. Only God knows the secret of the yud.

The Number Ten in Torah, Tradition, and the Human Body

The number ten is found throughout Torah and tradition, and in our bodies, providing constant hints to the One unifying Source in all reality.

God creates the world with ten utterances. God tests Avraham with ten trials. God redeems the Children of Israel from slavery through ten plagues. God reveals Himself to the Jewish people through ten commandments. God instructs Moses to build a tabernacle in the desert with ten curtains. God emanates creation into being through ten sefirot.

Ten also plays a role in Jewish practice. A traditional minyan is a group of ten men gathered together for prayer. There are ten days of תשובה *(t'shuvah)* return at the beginning of the Jewish new year. Yom Kippur, the holiest day of the year, is the tenth day of the new year.

Ten is also a prominent number in the human body. Our hands have ten fingers. Our feet, ten toes. The number that fills all reality with the secret of God's unity is physically represented in our bodies.

> **The hands of a person are aligned with the spiritual world, because the ten fingers are a hint to the ten lights** (Matok MiDvash, Zohar 3:186a).

The ten lights mentioned here are the ten sefirot, which we will study in the next section. The ten fingers of our hands hint to spiritual reality. Through the actions of our hands, we have the potential to reveal God's light in the world.

Sfat Emet sees a connection between God's hand and the ten sefirot:

> **Open Your hand and satisfy the desire of all living things** (Psalms 145:16).

Because די *(yad)* hand sounds like yud, Sfat Emet teaches:

> **Open Your hand can be read as open Your yud and satisfy the desire of all living things** (Sfat Emet, Chukat תרנ"ב ד"ה בעניו).

We pray that God will open His hand, His yud, the light of the ten sefirot, to satisfy creation with His goodness. We are meant to imitate God's hand by opening our own hands and bringing light to the world.

Deeper In: The Ten Sefirot

We will now take a little glimpse into the sefirot. The ten sefirot are so profoundly vast and deep that any amount of comprehension we may have of them is only a little bit. The sefirot are introduced in the Sefer Yetzirah, The Book of Creation.

> "The Sefer Yetzirah speaks of the Ten Sefirot as ten directions that constitute the totality of existence. These ten directions define a path to the Infinite Being who is beyond His creation" (Aryeh Kaplan, *Inner Space*, page 45).

> "The ten Sefirot taken together constitute a fundamental and all-inclusive Reality; moreover, the pattern of this Reality is organic, each of the Sefirot has a unique function, complements each of the others, and is essential for the realization or fulfillment of the others and of the whole. Because of their profound many-sidedness, the ten Sefirot seem to be shrouded in mystery" (Adin Steinsaltz, *The Thirteen Petalled Rose*, page 38).

What are the names of the ten sefirot?

> "There are indeed so many apparently unconnected levels of meaning to each ... a mere listing of their names does not adequately convey their essence" (Adin Steinsaltz, *The Thirteen Petalled Rose*, page 38).

Even though it does not convey their full essence, here is one way to translate the names of the sefirot: *Keter* Crown, *Chochmah* Wisdom, *Binah* Understanding, *Chesed* Love, *Gevurah* Restraint, *Tiferet* Beauty, *Netzach* Dominance, *Hod* Empathy, *Yesod* Foundation, and *Malchut* Kingship.

The Hebrew Letters of ספירה Sefirah

Playing with the word ספירה (*sefirah*), Rabbi Aryeh Kaplan teaches:

> "The term *Sefirah* (ספירה) itself derives or is related to the Hebrew *Saper* (ספר), meaning 'to express' or 'communicate,' and *Sapir* (ספיר), 'sapphire,' 'brilliance' or 'luminary.' It is also related to *Safar* (ספר) meaning 'number,' *Sefar* (ספר), 'boundary,' and *Sefer*, (ספר) 'book.' In essence, all of these are related concepts and point to the *Sefirot* as having two basic functions. First, the Sefirot are *Orot*, Lights or Luminaries that serve to reveal and express God's greatness. Secondly, they are *Kelim*, Vessels that limit and delineate God's infinite light, bringing it into the finite realm of number and boundary" (*Inner Space*, page 40).

> "It is through the *Sefirot* that God limits His infinite essence and manifests specific qualities that His creatures can grasp and relate to" (*Inner Space*, page 40).

Weaving all these meanings together, we can see the sefirot as God's illuminating, expressive book.

The traditional Torah scroll is called the ספר תורה (*sefer Torah*) book of Torah. All the books of Torah, as well as the commentaries of the sages, are called ספרים (*sefarim*) books. You very often find bookshelves filled with sefarim in Jewish homes, highlighting the essential place of learning in our lives. Through our sefarim the sefirot reveal God's light to the created world in a measured way.

Sefirot: One of God's Garments

Like many of our sages, Kedushat Levi teaches that it is not possible for creation to receive God's infinite essence directly, so God creates by dressing His essence in "garments."

We find the word שפע *(shefa)* abundance throughout kabbalistic and chassidic literature. It is referring to the abundant-divine-outpouring of life energy that God is giving the world at all times.

> **All worlds receive shefa from the Creator… and the worlds cannot receive shefa from Him, except through garments, and through many contractions, as is known from the words of Rabbi Yitzchak Luria, the Arizal. All the worlds are physical and dense compared to the shefa that comes from Him; even pure thought is thick and physical in relation to the Life force that is drawn from Him. Therefore, before creation, He created channels through which to give His shefa. Without this, creation could not bear the intensity of His shefa** (Kedushat Levi, B'reishit).

The garments and channels referred to here are the sefirot.

> **"The sefirot act variously as filters, garments or vessels for the light of the Eyn Sof [The infinite One] that fills them"** (Aryeh Kaplan, *Inner Space*, page 40).

This is not the first time I have written about God garmenting Himself in order to share His essence with creation. We have seen that God garments His essence in the Hebrew letters of the Torah. Now we see that God garments His essence in the ten sefirot. Which one is it? Hebrew, Torah, or sefirot? Of course, it is all of these. And more.

In the words of Sfat Emet:

> **All of creation is the garment of the divine** (Sfat Emet, Rosh Hashanah תרנ"ז ד"ה החיים).

Essence and Vessels

The great sages contemplated and wrote endlessly about God and His garments, which they referred to as עצמות *(atzmut)* essence and כלים *(kelim)* vessels. Atzmut refers to God, who is the essence of all that is. The vessels are the garments into which He contracts His essence, vessel after vessel, to move from the highest spiritual planes into all physical reality.

This movement from more expanded essence into more contracted vessels doesn't only happen between the Creator and His creation. It happens in every realm. It happens when a teacher teaches his student, when a mother nurses her baby. A good teacher's wisdom is more expansive than any student can absorb all at once, so the teacher must dress up ideas in language that can be understood by the student. A mother has more milk than her baby can receive at once, so the baby's adorable little mouth, perfectly shaped and designed, sucks just the right amount from a tiny opening in the nipple. As each vessel receives from its higher source, eventually it transforms into a source for future worlds. Students become teachers. Babies become mothers. And this way, like a divine waterfall, God's shefa continues to pour endlessly from the highest worlds into all worlds.

The Ten Sefirot and the Body

"The Sefirot thus constitute the inner structure and makeup of the Olamot-Universes" (Aryeh Kaplan, *Inner Space*, page 37).

Just as if we had purely spiritual eyes we would see in a jar of black ink a pool of illuminated yuds, if we had purely spiritual eyes we would see the ten sefirot underlying all of reality. All the tens of Torah and all the tens of our bodies hint to the inner, divine reality of the ten sefirot.

The sefirot are often divided into two groups. The upper three are qualities of consciousness and thought. The lower seven correspond to the world of action. The sefirot are often depicted by mapping them onto the human body, which is the place of consciousness and action. Not only do our fingers reflect the light of the sefirot, but our whole selves, the way we think and how we act, all reflect the sefirot. It is important to recognize that the sefirot are infinitely more expansive than where we locate them in the mind and body.

The Maharal teaches that the limbs of the body all have physical and spiritual reasons.

> **Of course the physical structure of the human being and the number of the limbs have physical purpose because they have activities to perform in the world. There is also a corresponding spiritual reality for every physical limb. It is about this spiritual reality that the Torah says, "And G-d created the human being in His image, in the image of God He created him"** (Be'er HaGolah, Be'er HaShishi).

Also Sfat Emet teaches that our bodies reflect the secrets of the image of God:

> The form of the body reflects the "form" of the soul (Sfat Emet, Ki Tetze תרנ"ח ד"ה במדרש).

The Raavad teaches:

> Everything that the Holy One created in His world corresponds to the human being, as it is written: Let us make the human being in our image and in our likeness. We can come to the hidden secrets of higher wisdom by contemplating the revealed creation, the human being (Raavid, Sefer Yetzirah 1:1).

Rabbi Abraham Meir ben Ibn Ezra teaches:

> The one who knows the secrets of his soul and the characteristics of his body can know the higher world, because the human being is a microcosm of all the worlds (Shmot 25:40).

By contemplating what we can know about ourselves, including our physical form, we can glimpse the dynamics of the ten sefirot.

Ten that are One

Even though the sefirot are divided into ten, each having its own name and quality, the sefirot are not essentially ten separate entities. Just like the yud is ten that is one, so too the sefirot are ten that are one. God is the connecting force unifying the sefirot.

In a teaching in the Zohar about the sefirot, Elijah the Prophet says:

> And You are the One who connects them and unifies them… and because You are within them anyone who separates one from another of the ten is considered as if he has made a separation in You (Tikunei Zohar, Patach Eliyahu).

Misperceiving the ten sefirot as separate entities is like creating a separation in God Himself.

Elijah tells us more:

> **With the sefirot You conceal Yourself from human beings.... And with the sefirot You direct both hidden and revealed worlds.** (Tikunei Zohar Patach Eliyahu)

God creates many worlds. Some of them are revealed and some are hidden. Revealed does not mean it is obvious to all. It means that it can potentially be discovered.

God conceals His essence in the ten sefirot. They are His hidden place. Paradoxically, God also reveals Himself through the sefirot. When we experience God's kindness, we are experiencing a revelation of the sefirah of Chesed. When we feel limitation, that is the sefirah of Gevurah.

Each sefirah has the qualities of all other sefirot within it. But at any given moment, one is dominant. Dominant but not absolute. There are qualities of limitation within loving kindness. There are elements of loving kindness in limitation. Remember, a loving mother doesn't give all her milk at once. An effective teacher doesn't overwhelm his students with all his knowledge. In essence, all the experiences of our lives are revelations of God's sefirot.

A Pictogram of the Sefirot

We now bring the sefirot into our study of the letter yud. Until now, we have understood yud as the raw material, the dimensionless point that begins all letters. But yud is also written as a highly defined, two-dimensional shape that looks like this:

Rabbi Mordechai Yaffe of Prague, the Baal HaLevushim, describes how the ten sefirot are hinted at in this well-defined yud.

> **The top left line of the letter points up to Keter. The body of the letter is Chochmah. The bottom left line of the letter points to Binah. The bottom right tail hints to Chesed, the first of the lower seven sefirot** (Levush Malchut, Levush HaT'chelet, Chapter 36).

God creates and interacts with creation through the Hebrew letters and the sefirot. Amazingly enough, the yud is both a Hebrew letter and a pictogram of the flow of the upper three sefirot into Chesed and the remaining lower sefirot. Like a waterfall, yud is the flow of the Divine into creation.

Yud in Aleph – Doorway into Creation

There are two ways to write aleph. The more common one is with two yuds (one upside down) and a diagonal vav.

Aleph is one, and hints to God's oneness. Aleph's three component letters, yud 10, vav 6, yud 10 equal 26. God's ineffable four-letter name, yud 10, heh 5, vav 6, heh 5 is also 26. With gematria we discover God's name in the letter aleph.

The Arizal had a different way of writing the aleph. He wrote it with a yud, a diagonal vav, and an upside down dalet — like this:

These three component letters spell יוד *(yud)*. Yud is hidden in the Arizal's aleph. Yud is aleph. Ten is One.

The upper yud that is Higher wisdom is connected through the vav connection to the dalet. The letter ד *(dalet)* spelled out can be read as דלת *(delet)* doorway. The Arizal's aleph depicts the yud of God's higher wisdom coming down into the doorway of creation.

How the fiery aleph that I fell in love with as a little girl continues to delight and illuminate my mind and soul!

A Waterfall of Light

Now that I have talked for a long time and you have listened for a long time, we begin to glimpse the meaning of Sarai being the שׂר *(sar)* master of the י *(yud)*. Sarai is the first doorway, a human portal for all we conceptualize yud to be. She is the flow of the light of the Eyn Sof into creation.

> **Sarah was not separated from the essence of life for even one moment. She continually drew down an abundant flow of new illuminations, from one level to the next, all the years of her life** (Sfat Emet, Chayei Sarah תרל״ב ד״ה במדרש).

Sarah's holy waterfall of light shines forever.

> The illuminations of the righteous ones who draw down life to the world remain forever, because every impression that holiness makes in the world remains. The righteous are called alive even when they have passed, because their life force still illuminates the world (Sfat Emet, Chayei Sarah תרנ״א ד״ה במדרש).

What does it mean that Sarah's light shines forever? Is the world always illuminated by holy light?

Sarai Shares Her Yud

Right before Avram and Sarai conceive Yitzchak, God changes both of their names.

> You shall no longer be called אברם *(Avram)*, but your name shall be אברהם *(Avraham)*, for I will make you the father of a multitude of nations (B'reishit 17:3-6).

> As for your wife Sarai, you shall not call her שרי *(Sarai)*, but her name shall be שרה *(Sarah)*. I will bless her, and I will give you a son by her. I will bless her so that she shall give rise to nations; rulers of peoples shall issue from her (B'reishit 17:15-16).

Playing with the letters, we see that Sarai's yud, which is ten in gematria, splits into two hehs, five and five.

> The Holy One took the yud from שרי *(Sarai)* and divided it into two, half for שרה *(Sarah)* and half for אברהם *(Avraham)* (Midrash Rabbah, B'reishit 47).

First Sarai shares the yud with Avram. Then

> **The two hehs connect as one and give birth to higher worlds** (Zohar 1:96a).

That higher world is revealed through יצחק *(Yitzchak)*.

> יצחק *(Yitzchak)* passes the yud to
>
> יעקב *(Yaakov)* whose name changes to
>
> ישראל *(Yisrael)* who is eventually called
>
> ישורון *(Yeshurun)*

The Jewish people are called

> יהודים *(Yehudim)* Jews.

The story of the Jewish people inheriting and passing on Sarah's yud from one generation to the next is found in the Yiddish expression dos pintale yid, the little yid. Yid is short for יהודי *(Yehudi)* Jew. It is also the letter yud. Yid and yud are essentially the same thing. The pintale yid-yud is the Jewishness, the nekudah hapnimit, the essential point of connection to God. It is the Jewish soul.

Sarah's holy yud must constantly be shared. Her illuminations remain forever in the world, but her light needs to be revealed by each of us.

Sarah was spiritually awake to the light of God every moment of her life. Like Sarah, we too have the potential to wake up spiritually every day and reveal the light.

> **God gives a point of awakening to each person of Israel, every day, to attach to Him** (Sfat Emet, Chayei Sarah תרל"ג ד"ה במדרש).

Sometimes we are awake to our pintale yid. Sometimes we are asleep. But whether we are aware of it or not,

> **God guards this inner point so that it will remain within the Children of Israel** (Sfat Emet, Chanukah תרל"א ד"ה זאת חנוכה).

He Will Laugh

Sarah and Avraham both laughed when God told them the time had come to bring their long-promised child into the world.

> **And Avraham fell on his face ויצחק *(vayitzchak)* and he laughed, and he said in his heart: Will a hundred-year-old man father a child? And will Sarah, who is ninety, give birth?** (B'reishit 17:17)

> **ותצחק *(Vatizchak)* And Sarah laughed within herself, saying: After I am worn out will I have pleasure with my husband so old?** (B'reishit 18:12)

In Hebrew grammar, a yud at the beginning of a verb signifies future tense. יצחק (*Yitzchak*) means he will laugh. Along with pointing to the inner divine essence of reality, the yud in Yitzchak's name points to a future of laughter.

Every Jewish parent is touched with a bit of prophecy when naming their child. How much more so the prophet who names his child.

> **And Avraham called the name of his son that was born to him, that Sarah birthed to him, יצחק *(Yitzchak)*, he will laugh** (B'reishit 21:3).

Yitzchak's name is a prophecy of the future of the Jewish people — a future of holy, redemptive laughter. King David wrote that all the tears shed during our thousands of years of difficult history will bring forth joy.

> **Those who sow in tears will reap in joy** (Psalms 126:5).

Laughter in the Land of Israel

King David knew that the future of laughter will be in the Land of Israel.

> **When God returns our captives to Zion, we will be like dreamers. Then our mouths will be full of laughter and our tongues will be full of joy** (Psalms 126:1-2).

Yitzchak was born in the Land of Israel. He was the only one of the three patriarchs who was never outside its borders. In the story of Avraham and Sarah's move to Israel, there is a hint that Yitzchak had an essential connection to the land, even before he was born.

We often think that the journey of the Jewish people to Israel begins when God told Avraham:

> **Go from your land, from your birthplace, from your father's home to the land that I will show you** (B'reishit 12:1).

But it actually begins a few verses before that, right after we hear:

> **And Sarai was עקרה *(akara)*, she had no child** (B'reishit 11:30).

The very next verse is:

> **And Terach took Avram, his son, and Lot, the son of Charan,**

and Sarai, his daughter-in-law, the wife of Avram his son, and they went out together from Ur Kasdim to go to the land of Canaan, and they came to Charan and they settled there (B'reishit 11:31).

Why did Terach take his family and move? The Torah does not tell us.

Until this point in the Torah, no one had chosen to uproot themselves from their birthplace. Adam and Eve, Noah and his family, and the generation of the Tower of Bavel had all been uprooted, but not by choice. Uprooting a family and moving to a new land has never been easy. When people move, they have good reasons.

Once again, the word עקרה *(akara)* provides a hint. As well as meaning barren, uproot, and essence, akara, as the verb לעקור *(la'akor)*, implies to move from one place to another. Looking for connections between words and verses that are next to each other in the Torah, we notice that right after we hear that Sarah is akara, the move to the Land of Israel begins.

I suggest that we can now understand: "And Sarah was עקרה *(akara)*", this way:

Sarai was the essential catalyst for uprooting and moving the family. She knew that she was going to be the mother of the Jewish people. She knew that her long-promised child, the first fruit of the blossoming Jewish people, needed to be born and raised in the Land of Israel, the place of future laughter, the land of he will laugh.

9
The Land that I Will Show You

Torah is also the ongoing story of the Jewish people that is still being written. My story, your story, the story of our children and beyond, are ever-expanding chapters of Torah. HERE I SHARE PART OF my story.

I know that uprooting and moving to a new land is not easy, because I also uprooted myself and moved to a new land. I moved from Minnesota to Israel.

I was seventeen when I first came to Israel on a youth-group tour. Seventeen is the gematria of the word טוב *(tov)* good. Seventeen was a good age to come to the good land.

Throughout the Torah, the Land of Israel is called ארץ טובה *(eretz tovah)* a good land. When God first tells Moses that He will bring the Children of Israel to the Land of Israel, He describes it as:

> **A good and expansive land, a land flowing with milk and honey** (Shmot 3:8).

After leading the Jewish people for forty years through the desert, Moses looks out over the land and says:

> **The Lord, your God, is bringing you to a good land, a land flowing with water and springs and fountains coming forth from plains and hills. A land of wheat and barley and grapes and figs and pomegranates, a land of olive oil and honey** (D'varim 8:7).

Moses was not allowed to enter the Land of Israel. But by the great miracle of being born at a good time, the time when the prophecies of the Jewish people returning to our land are coming true, God brought me to Israel.

Everyone in my family loves Israel and has been here many times to visit. But no one ever talked about moving to Israel. And yet, from the moment I stepped off the plane and onto the land, I knew this was my place. A few years into living here, I heard a voice speaking to me from within the cells of my own body, saying:

> **את במקום הנכון** *(at b'makom hanachon)* You are in the right place (my own inner Hebrew voice).

For a time, that inner voice spoke these reassuring, loving words to me clearly, audibly, again and again, day and night. My soul welcomed me home in her native tongue, articulating what I knew from my first moment in Israel.

I didn't yet know the secrets in the words that my soul spoke. Now I know that God is called מקום *(Makom)* place. The letters of מקום also make up the word קיום *(kiyum)* existence. The letters are also found in the verb לקום *(lakum)* to rise up. With my expanding understanding of מקום *(Makom)*, I now hear:

You are in the right Makom, a place of rising up to a fuller existence, a life in God's place.

I knew I would live here, that my future was here. But how could it be? My family, who I love and am very attached to, would not be coming with me. How could I possibly leave them?!

When I first came to Israel, I did not know the words that God said to Avraham:

> **Go from your land, from your birthplace, from your father's home to the land that I will show you** (B'reishit 12:1).

But I began to live those words.

Sfat Emet asks:

> **Why doesn't God reveal to Avraham immediately where he is going?** (Sfat Emet, Lech Lecha תרל״ב ברש״י ד״ה)

His answer is that, by calling Israel "the land that I will show you," God is telling Avraham where he is going. He is going to the land of continual divine revelation. The more one lives in the land and seeks for God, the more is revealed.

I spent the six weeks of that youth-group tour with my eyes and ears eagerly watching out for everything God was showing me. I always took a window seat on the bus so I could turn my head and put my forehead on the window. I wanted to focus on the miracles, the history, the challenges, the beauty.

But something was being revealed to me beyond what my eyes could see or my ears could hear. I felt the soul of Israel beginning to be revealed to me. I have now spent more than forty years watching out with my heart and soul for everything that God continues to show me.

It will not come as a surprise that one of the things that delighted me most on that first trip to Israel was that the fiery Hebrew of the Torah and prayer book was now everywhere — on the street signs, in conversations around me, on the radio, in shops. Children were speaking Hebrew. On Fridays the bus drivers would say, "Shabbat shalom." Surrounded by Hebrew, I was as happy as a kid in a Hebrew candy store!

One of my favorite love-of-Hebrew stories is from the time I got my appendix out. When the anesthesiologist told me, in Hebrew of course, to count down from ten to one, I gleefully announced to my roommate Maya, who was still standing at the doorway of the operating room, "I am getting my appendix out in Hebrew!"

Children of the Future

LIKE SARAH, WHO KNEW THAT Yitzchak had to be born in Israel, some wise place in my soul knew that my future child needed to be born here. Kalya is the first sabra in our family in two thousand years. I had no idea what it would be like to raise a child here. It was uncharted territory. With each stage I understand more profoundly why I, like Sarah, uprooted myself to move here. It dawned on me recently that it might have been Kalya's soul, long before she was born, that propelled me to make aliyah, so she could live here. Raising Kalya in Israel has given me a glimpse of the future of laughter in the land.

Field Trips to Holiness

To become a child of the future it is essential for us to be rooted in our past. There are hints to the essential link between past and future in the word קדם (*kedem*) ancient, primordial past. ק (*Kuf*) ד (*dalet*) ם (*mem*) are also the root letters of להתקדם (*l'hitkadem*) to move forward, to progress. קדם is also in the description of God as קדמונו של עולם (*kadmono shel olam*) The Ancient One of the world. Weaving these meanings together, we can understand God to be The Ancient One who moves the world forward.

With these hinted meanings, the verse:

חדש ימינו כקדם (*chadesh yameinu k'kedem*)

which is usually translated as:

Renew our days as of old (Lamentations 5:21)

can also be understood as:

Move our days toward a renewing future.

So, which one is it? Do we long to renew our past — or move to a new future? Of course it is both. Rooted in our past, we move forward, aligned with The Ancient Future One.

One of the blessings of growing up in Israel is that children are rooted in their past as they grow into their future. When Kalya was in first grade she went on a field trip to the Kotel, the (Western) Wall. The Kotel is the retaining wall that stood on the west side of the second Temple in Jerusalem.

To appreciate the significance of Kalya's field trip to the Kotel, I need first to take you on a historical field trip to Jerusalem and show you at least a little something about the בית המקדש (*Beit HaMikdash*) The House of Holiness — The Temple.

There were two Temples in Jerusalem. The first Temple was built during King Solomon's reign, between 970 and 930 BCE. It was destroyed by Nebuchadnezzar, the King of Babylonia, in 586 BCE. The second Temple was built at the time of Ezra and Nechemiah by Jews who returned from the Babylonian exile in 516 BCE. In the first century CE, King Herod built the retaining wall and renovated the second Temple. It was destroyed by the Romans in 70 CE.

For a thousand years the Temple in Jerusalem was the center of life for the Jewish people. It was the center because God's life-giving presence was revealed there.

> **When the Temple existed, it was a revealed reality that all life comes from God** (Sfat Emet, Chanukah תרל״א ד״ה כתיב).

Every detail of the Temple's construction had spiritual meaning. For example, the windows were designed so light would shine from inside the Temple outwards. This hinted to the Temple being the source of God's spiritual illumination, not only for the Jewish people but for the whole world.

> **When the Temple existed, it was revealed that Life went out to the whole world from there** (Sfat Emet, Chanukah תרל״ב ד״ה נודע).

Ever since the destruction of the second Temple, longing for Jerusalem, which includes longing for the Temple, has occupied us day and night. We pray for Jerusalem three times a day. We pray for Jerusalem in the blessing after eating bread. In the blessing after eating one of the seven species of the Land of Israel, (wheat, barley, grapes, figs, pomegranates, olives, and dates), we say:

> **Rebuild Jerusalem, Your holy city, speedily in our days, and raise us up within it, and make us joyful with its rebuilding,**

and may we eat of its fruit, and be satisfied with its goodness.
(Blessing after eating of the seven species).

Just imagine: Everywhere in the world, for thousands of years, when Jews ate a grape or a piece of cake they prayed to be lifted up to a joyful life in a rebuilt Jerusalem.

I once asked a Jewish woman who was born and raised in Ethiopia what place Jerusalem had in her childhood. Her answer was that Jerusalem was always in everyone's mind. As well as being constantly part of their prayers, it was regularly a part of their ordinary conversations. When she did something naughty, the admonishment from her parents was, "You won't go to Jerusalem if you do that."

Jerusalem and B'reishit

In truth, the centrality of Jerusalem precedes even the times of the Temple. It goes back to the beginning, to בראשית (b'reishit).

Divided into two words, we have:

ברא *(barah)* He created

שית *(sheet)* foundation — ש *(shin)*, ת *(tav)* are the root letters of תשתית *(tashtit)* foundation.

> The Mishna teaches that there was a stone in the Holy of Holies called שתייה *(shetiyah)* foundation (Mishna Yoma 5:2).
>
> It was called foundation because the foundation of the world was from there (Babylonian Talmud, Yoma 54b).

The Zohar teaches:

> The world was not created until God took a stone, called the foundation stone, and threw it into the depths, and from it the world expanded. It is the center point of the world, and on this spot stood the Holy of Holies (Zohar 1:231a).

In Midrash Tanchuma we find:

> The Land of Israel sits at the center of the world, Jerusalem in the center of the Land of Israel, the Temple in the center of Jerusalem, the Ark (in the Holy of Holies) in the center of the Temple, and in front of the Ark, the foundation stone, from which the world was founded (Kedoshim 10).

Now we have a Talmud–Zohar–Midrash-informed interpretation of the first verse of Torah:

God created the foundation of the world, placing a stone in the Holy of Holies, and from there He created the heavens and the earth.

For the past two thousand years there have always been a few very brave souls who managed to make the difficult pilgrimage to the Kotel in Jerusalem. But for most, Jerusalem lived only in their prayers, poetry, and dreams.

WE NOW RETURN TO KALYA'S field trip to the Kotel. Rooted in her past, Kalya, together with her sweet six-year-old friends, went to the place where they could hear the ancient heartbeat of their own people, the place where creation began, where God's presence is revealed on earth.

Moving toward the future of laughter, Kalya's life in Israel continues to be an ongoing answer to the prayers of her ancestors.

Glimpses of Our Razah D'Echad

THE BLESSINGS OF LIVING IN Israel are not always as obvious and awesome as going on a field trip to the Kotel. There are so many blessings in everyday interactions. If I had to choose one word to describe the essence of life in Israel, it would be קשר *(kesher)* connection. There is an undeniable feeling of being connected to everyone, of being responsible for everyone, whether you know them or not, whether you agree with them or not, whether you like them or not.

As it says in the Talmud:

> **All of Israel are ערבים *(arevim)* interconnected and responsible for each other** (Babylonian Talmud, Shavuot 39a).

The word ערב *(arev)* also means sweet.

Here are a few sweet stories of our interconnectedness.

Once I was driving with Kalya in the car when she was a baby. I stopped at a red light and heard several loud honks from a big truck next to me. I turned and saw that the truck driver was urging me to open my window. When I opened my window, he shouted: "שמש על התינוקת" *(Shemesh al hatinoket)* There's sun on the baby!" I loved the fact that this truck driver was very concerned that there was too much sun on my baby. He clearly really cared.

Kalya never felt cold as a little girl. Even when it was cold outside, she would never agree to put on a sweater or jacket. She insisted on walking to school with only her favorite short-sleeved blue T-shirt. There was hardly a day when someone didn't call out to us from their car or from the street, "לא קר לילדה ?" *(Lo kar l'yalda?)* Isn't the girl cold?"

Some people in Israel get annoyed at these very common occurrences of "strangers" getting involved in their lives by offering unsolicited advice. But they delight me.

Sweet Sounds on the Train up to Jerusalem

RECENTLY I RETURNED TO ISRAEL from a long visit in Minnesota. The train up to Jerusalem was very quiet, a blessing after a long flight. After a few moments I heard a very beautiful, quiet, sweet sound. I hadn't heard a sound even remotely like it in all my months outside of Israel. The religious man next to me was studying Talmud, sweetly singing-chanting-praying the words he was learning. His Torah song was a holy sound that went directly to my soul. It was the "still small voice" of God that Eliyahu the prophet speaks of, welcoming me back to this מקום *(makom)* place that God keeps showing me (Kings 1 19:12).

It struck me at that moment that, much as I might try, when I am outside of Israel I cannot accurately describe what it is like to live here. A library of books, a thousand podcasts, cannot convey what this timeless, sweet sound of Torah on the train up to Jerusalem communicated in an instant.

I was about to tell this Talmud singer how beautiful and welcoming the sound of his learning was, especially after being out of the country for a while, when the young man sitting across from us asked him if he would share what he was learning. I immediately chimed in with, "Yes, I would love to learn with you too." The Talmud singer looked at me a bit surprised. From the way I was dressed, he probably wouldn't have expected me to be eager to learn Talmud with him. I was wearing pants, which many religious women don't wear. The young man across from us also wasn't dressed in typical religious clothing.

But he kindly agreed to learn with us, and for the rest of the train ride up to Jerusalem we had a lovely time learning Talmud together. He was pleasantly surprised that both of us had experience in Talmud study and could offer clear ideas on intricate topics. As we ascended the hills to Jerusalem, we were learning about the offerings that were brought in the Temple when the Jews would ascend to Jerusalem on the pilgrimage festivals. In particular, we were learning about the joy offering. I was overwhelmed by a sweet joy that I offered to God for raising me up again to this good land.

From the time of Sarah and Avraham, the Jewish people have existed as one body and one soul, called the רזה דאחד *(razah d'echad)* secret of oneness. For me, these expressions of caring and connection are sightings of the beautiful inner face, the sheina punim, of our razah d'echad. I experience them as tangibly as the lovely sensation of the first warm sun after a long, cold winter.

On one of her visits to Israel, my niece Eliana picked up the scent of our secret oneness quickly. At the end of her first day of visiting us in Jerusalem, she said, "I can see why you live here." When I asked her why, she said, "Everyone is so connected to each other here. I felt it all day long."

Piecing Together Our Secret Oneness Puzzle

In Israel, our razah d'echad is not always obvious, especially if your main source of information is the news. We have dozens of political parties that argue vehemently about every aspect of our society. We have tremendous religious and cultural diversity.

Like everything else in Torah, not being obvious does not mean it is not real. It means it is hidden and we must discover it. Oneness does not mean we are all the same or all meant to agree. Having different opinions does not contradict our razah d'echad. The opposite: All the different opinions are essential pieces in our secret-oneness puzzle.

One great example of this is the Talmud, the enormous sea of disagreements between the Rabbis. Even though they disagreed, the Rabbis in the Talmud always listened to and thoroughly understood each other's ideas. The house of Hillel and the house of Shammai were known for always holding different opinions. Even so, Hillel had such respect for Shammai that he always presented Shammai's opinion before his own.

The Jewish soul is like a puzzle. Each of us has a unique shape and design that is essential to the whole picture.

> **Everyone has a unique part, and even so we are all deeply connected as one whole** (Sfat Emet, Shmot ואלה ה"ד ז"תרנ).

Our Soul and the Hebrew Letters

> ישראל *(Yisrael)* Israel is an acronym for יש שישים ריבוא אותיות לתורה *(Yesh shishim ribo otiot laTorah)* There are 600,000 letters in the Torah. Correspondingly, there are 600,000 root souls of Israel (Zohar Chadash, Shir HaShirim 91a).

> Each one of us is aligned with a letter of Torah. Each soul derives its nature from its particular letter of Torah. Each soul is a certain personification of Godliness. When we speak a letter of the Torah with devotion, that letter comprises the totality of Torah. And every letter is essential to manifesting the whole. And just as a sefer Torah missing even a single letter is invalid, so each soul is essential to Israel (Meor Einayim, Chukat, Zot HaTorah).

In exile, the pieces of our unified soul were scattered all over the world. In exile, we cannot see the whole picture.

Sfat Emet teaches that exile separates our hearts.

> The essence of exile is when the hearts of the Children of Israel cannot gather as one. That is why we pray: Gather our dispersed ones from the four corners of the earth (Sfat Emet, VaYechi תרמ"ב ד"ה האספו).

Our sages call this current time of gathering in Israel:

ראשית צמיחת גאולתנו *(reishit tzimchat geulateinu)* The beginning of the flowering of our redemption.

We are beginning to gather together our dispersed hearts to reveal our unified soul, our soul that was in God's mind even before creation. Patience please! We are putting our secret-Hebrew letter-oneness puzzle together. When all our pieces come together, with each of us contributing our own essential shape and design, the whole picture will be revealed.

> In the future, the Oneness that is within creation will be clarified, and this is called razah d'echad. But now it is a hidden secret, higher than we can comprehend. And although we do not comprehend this, we must believe it (Sfat Emet, VaYigash תרל״ה ד״ה בזמר).

A New Reishit

EARLIER I WROTE THAT NO one in my family ever talked about living in Israel. But, as it turns out, some were dreaming about it.

When I first moved to Israel I got a letter from my brother-in-law, Mark, telling me that he thought I was very brave to make aliyah and that he too deeply believed in living here. And if he were brave enough, he would do the same. Although we never spoke again about this letter, I never forgot Mark's powerful words.

That was forty years ago. Five years ago I got a phone call from Mark telling me that he and my sister Laura were coming to visit for Passover. I was overjoyed. Having my family visit me in Israel has always made me enormously happy. But then, at the end of the conversation, he said something that stunned me.

Here is our conversation:

Mark, speaking calmly: "We want to spend a few extra days in Israel, because we want to look at real estate."

My mouth drops open. I am astonished. Silent. And then I say: "Mark?!!! What are you talking about!? Are you talking about buying a house in Israel?"

Mark: "Yes. I have never given up my dream of living in Israel."

That moment was the beginning of a new reishit in my life — Laura and Mark making aliyah! After forty years, is it possible that I would now share life in Israel with my family?!

Yes!

Like Sarah, who laughed hearing the miraculous news that she was going to have a baby, I laughed hearing the miraculous news that my sister and brother-in-law were coming to join me in Israel. This was not ordinary laughter. It was holy laughter. The laughter of tears transforming to joy. The laughter of a dream coming true. The elevated laughter that King David spoke of.

> **A song of ascents. When God will return the captivity of Zion, we will be like dreamers. Then our mouth will be full of laughter, and our tongues joyful** (Psalms 126:1).

The land of future laughter danced in my heart.

Here is Laura and Mark's aliyah story in Laura's words:

Laura and Mark's Story

Turning right off The Founders Street in Zichron Yaakov, I enter the little alley that leads to my new home. The house on the corner of the alley is almost hidden behind the display of colorful flowers, teapots, guitars, and posters with Hebrew poetry displayed along the length of its fence. I can hardly believe that this is the street where I live.

As I enter the alley, I catch a glimpse of a little redheaded four-year-old, Estie, in front of her house. She sees me and her eyes light up as she sprints toward me, arms held up high. "Laura, Laura," she calls, as she launches herself into my arms, wrapping her arms and legs around me for a full minute of unabashed affection. Then she breaks free and starts skipping back toward her older brother Yossie, who more shyly approaches for his hug and greeting.

Two houses down, another neighbor's daughter, Hadassah, also four, and as pretty as can be, steps out of her house dressed in her white Shabbat dress. Imitating the more outgoing Estie, she also calls out my name and then jumps into my arms for a huge hug.

These little heart-warmers are just part of the incredible community we have found ourselves thrown into as new olim (new citizens of Israel).

For the twelve-and-a-half years prior to our arrival in Israel, my husband and I circumnavigated the globe in our sailboat. We saw so many amazing places, spending days, weeks, and even months in countries that we got to know and love. We began our trip in Rhode Island, on the east coast of the United States. From there we sailed to the Caribbean, through the Panama Canal, and across the Pacific Ocean to the many enchanting islands of the South Pacific. We continued to New Zealand, Australia, Indonesia, Malaysia, Singapore, and Thailand. We shipped our boat to Turkey to avoid a particularly hazardous route. From there we sailed to Israel, Greece, Italy, and Spain before heading through Gibraltar and down to the Canary Islands. From there we crossed the Atlantic Ocean to return through the Caribbean to our starting point in Rhode Island.

At each stop we thought about whether we could live long term in that place. Although we fell in love with many places, we realized we could never feel at home in any of them, save one. After seeing so much of the world, we knew the only place we would ever really feel at home would be Israel.

On a visit to Zichron Yaakov, a coastal town just south of Haifa, in the spring of 2020, as Covid was raging around the world, we found a simple house with a view so splendid it took our breath away. We knew it was the place for us and we bought it.

Shortly afterward we went to visit my sister Diane and her husband, Jonathan, in Jerusalem. Avid Israeli folk dancers, they wanted to celebrate by showing us the dance that was created for Idan Reichel's song "B'reishit." The dance was so moving and beautiful! I could catch some of the words, but immediately wanted to know what all of them meant. As we went through the text, line by line, tears flowed down my face. It seemed as if that song had been written especially for us.

"Someone is waiting for you at home. Close to here, maybe in some corner. A place you will call home. And when you enter it, it will become yours."

The song seemed to allude to the finding of an earth-bound home, rather than one at sea:

"She (love) waited for the good earth, as she had for the sea."

After nearly thirteen years of wandering the globe in our ever-transient, ever-changing home on a boat, a place was calling to us, a place well-rooted on the land that would become our home, for as far in the future as we could envision.

From our first day in Zichron, we were welcomed with open arms by our neighbors, willing to help in any way possible. While we were waiting for our shipment from the U.S. to arrive, they brought us beds, tables, and chairs. They baked us challahs, cakes, and cookies and invited us for coffee and Shabbat meals. The local Rabbi helped put up our mezuzot.

It became a regular thing, particularly on Friday afternoons, to hear a knock on our door and to open it only to find two or even three little ones coming for a visit and some cookies. On one visit, Yossie brought along some change and wanted to put it in my tzedakah (charity) box. When I informed him that I did not have one, he and his sister were flabbergasted. A few hours later, upon returning from an afternoon stroll, we found Estie and Yossie waiting for us at our door, proudly holding the new tzedakah box they had made for us. Now we could fill it with coins and give it to the Rabbi, as they instructed us.

My husband and I are not religious, and we have been haphazard in our observance of Shabbat over the years. Now Shabbat is the centerpoint of our week. Starting with the arrival of Diane and Jonathan, who came to live in Zichron (from Jerusalem) for two months in order to be close to us during our first year as new immigrants, our Shabbats quickly evolved from being pleasant but fairly isolated affairs to large, warm, family celebrations. Not a Shabbat went by without several guests. Our kitchen table, which we had brought from the U.S., was suddenly way too small to accommodate everyone. But it didn't matter, as the closeness at the table was just part of the fun. Shopping for Shabbat on Thursday afternoon and Friday morning became a pleasant excursion with lots of thought going into the feast I wanted to prepare. The actual meal preparation was easier and more fun than cooking had ever been for me, with so much help from my sister, my niece, my cousin, and all their respective partners. Each Shabbat has been special in its own way, depending on who was visiting that week. An occasional drop-by visit from neighbors added to the festive feeling. Whereas Shabbat in the U.S. always felt like a day when there was so much one could not do, in Israel, in our new home, it has become a day when there are an amazing number of lovely things one gets to do.

Our Names

LIVING OUR LIVES, WE ARE always writing the long-hand version of our names. Our lives become our book. It takes a long time to clarify our names and write our books. After living my life for sixty-four years and writing this book for twelve, I will share a few stories now being revealed in my family's Hebrew names.

My name is Dena Rachel. My sister Laura's Hebrew name is Leah Yanite. In the Torah, Leah is Rachel's older sister. Laura is my older sister. Some teach that Leah and Rachel were twins. Laura and I have been asked many times if we are twins. Rachel and Leah were the two wives of Jacob. Dena was the daughter of Leah and Jacob, the niece of Rachel. From every perspective, our names connect us to Jacob. No wonder Laura and Mark chose to live in Zichron Yaakov, Memory of Jacob!

Jacob, the third patriarch of the Jewish people, spent many years in exile and then returned to the Land of Israel. Sfat Emet teaches that through Jacob we learn how to maintain our Jewish identity in exile and eventually return to our land.

Mark's Hebrew name is Moshe Mordechai. Moses (Moshe) longed for forty years to enter the promised land, but never did. Mark longed to be in Israel for at least forty years. In the book of Esther, Mordechai lived in Persia at the time the Jews were beginning to return after the seventy-year Babylonian exile. Now, after an even longer exile, the Jews are returning to Israel again. And Mark has returned with them.

That miraculous Passover four years ago when Laura and Mark stunned me by coming to Israel to look for a home, we drove up to Zichron Yaakov. We parked in a spot that "happened" to be available. When we got out of the car, I noticed a Hebrew sign engraved on the wall exactly where we parked. Again, I was speechless. It said:

> **We have come to the land of our fathers with a holy purpose. We have no other home in all of the world. Here we will live and here we will die** (Meir Lev Harashko, from the early pioneers in the land).

Laura and Mark found no other home in the entire world. But "someone was waiting for them at home." In Zichron Yaakov, in Memory of Jacob, they returned home and found their family, and all their ancestors, waiting for them.

Rachel's Spiritual Watchtower

I WAS NAMED DENA IN memory of my great-grandmother on my father's side. I wasn't named Rachel after anyone in the immediate family. But of course, by naming me Rachel, my parents, with the touch of prophecy that all parents are given, engraved in me an essential connection to the matriarch Rachel.

Rachel, the beloved wife of Jacob, died when she was on her way to the Land of Israel with Jacob and all the family, after Jacob's twenty-year exile in Charan. She was not buried in the Cave of Machpelah with all the other ancestors. She was buried on the road to Ephrat.

The Midrash explains why Rachel was buried in this place.

> **Why did Jacob, our father, bury Rachel on the road to Ephrat? Jacob saw that, in the future, the Children of Israel would pass by there on their way into exile. He buried her there so she would pray to God to be compassionate with Israel in exile** (Midrash Rabbah, B'reishit 82:10).

Rachel's lonely roadside burial place became her spiritual watchtower. For thousands of years Rachel has watched over, wept, and prayed for her children who are scattered all over the world. She refuses to be consoled until they return home.

> **There is a voice heard on high, of wailing, of bitter weeping. Rachel is weeping for her children. She refuses to be comforted for her children who are gone** (Jeremiah 31:15).

Through the prophet Jeremiah, God assures Rachel that a time of great comfort will come.

> **Restrain your voice from weeping and your eyes from tears…. There is hope for your future, says God, and your children will return to their boundaries** (Jeremiah 31:16).

That time of comfort has begun. We, the scattered people of Israel, are returning to our boundaries. Perhaps now, Rachel's tears are beginning to subside.

My Connection to Rachel

FOR MORE THAN FORTY YEARS I have been constructing my own spiritual watchtower. Like the world God created with the higher wisdom of Torah, my spiritual watchtower is built, letter by letter, word by word, verse by verse, teacher by teacher, book by book, of Torah wisdom. My watchtower is not a fortress that separates me from the world. It connects me to the world, especially to Jewish people who live outside of Israel.

I, like Rachel, live on the road between Israel and the diaspora. I am a Torah teacher, and when I learn Torah I often have my mind and heart turned to family, friends, and students, many of whom live outside of Israel. My notebooks are filled with the names of the people I think would be inspired, uplifted, guided, or comforted by a particular teaching. I travel often to the United States to teach students who are thirsty for the deep Torah that flows like water in Jerusalem.

Technology has made it possible for me to teach classes on Sfat Emet from my home. I call the course *Torah from Jerusalem*. Sfat Emet wanted his teachings to reach every Jew. He lived at a time when women, for the most part, were not Torah teachers. I often wonder what Sfat Emet would say if he saw me teaching his wisdom to students all over the world from my Jerusalem watchtower. I truly believe he would be delighted.

There is יש No End אין סוף

Beginnings contain the whole. The Torah begins with the letter ב *(bet)*. Bet's two component letters, ד *(dalet)* 4 and ו *(vav)* 6, equal י *(yud)* 10. Hidden in the ב *(bet)* of בראשית *(b'reishit)* in the beginning of the beginning, is the yud, the soul of Israel.

We identify ב *(bet)* with the word ברכה *(bracha)* blessing. The letter is open in the front. The bet is the source of blessing and beckons us to move toward a future of blessing.

With atbash, ת *(tav)*, the last letter of the alephbet, transforms to א *(aleph)*, the first letter. The end becomes a new beginning.

Our lives are chapters in the endlessly revealing Torah of the אין סוף *(Eyn Sof)* The Endless One. This is the last chapter of my book to date. My new reishit is being lived as I write it. It is being written as I live it.

Sitting on Laura and Mark's porch, looking out over the greening, flowering, spring hills of the Carmel Mountain range in Northern Israel, Rav Kook's poem comes alive.

> **And a generation will yet arise, full of life,**
> **And draw delight unending from the dew of heaven,**
> **And this people, returned to life, will hear the wealth of life's secrets from the vistas of the Carmel and the Sharon,**
> **And from the delight of song and life's beauty,**
> **A holy light will abound**
> (Orot HaRaAyah, Whispers of Existence).

Rooted in our ancient-present-future story we are together again, growing into a Tree of Life, reaching up to touch higher worlds, reaching up to touch heaven.

10
Our Sages and Sources
Written and Selected by Rabbi Dov Laimon

Sefer Yetzirah
The Most Ancient of all Mystical Texts

Sefer Yetzirah is an ancient mystical text that introduces the thirty-two paths of wisdom. Those thirty-two paths correspond to the combination of the twenty-two letters of the Hebrew alephbet and the ten sefirot. The Talmud attributes Sefer Yetzirah to Avraham.

> Ten Sefirot of Nothingness. Their end is imbedded in their beginning, and their beginning in their end, like a flame in a burning coal. For the Master is singular. He has no second. And before One, what do you count? (Sefer Yetzirah 1:7)

The Zohar
First Century CE

The Zohar, The Book of Radiance, is the primary text of the Jewish mystical tradition. Kabbalists in every generation have plumbed its depths. It contains the teachings of Rabbi Shimon bar Yochai, Rashbi, offered to a select group of students, including his son Elazar. Rabbi Shimon was a student of Rabbi Akiva in the first century. The Zohar is organized according to the weekly Torah portions. Recently the publication of the entire Zohar into English by Professor Danny Matt has greatly benefited the English-speaking world.

> **Rabbi Shimon elaborated the verse "And I will place my words in your mouth"** (Isaiah 51:16). **How great it is for a person to learn Torah day and night and come to new understanding. Every authentic expression of Torah forms a new heavenly realm. For just as all existence is created with the letters of Torah, so too one who studies in holiness and purity contributes to creation with his words and his letters of Torah** (Zohar 1:4b).

Tikunei Zohar
First Century CE

Tikunei Zohar is distinct from Sefer HaZohar. Tradition tells us that Tikunei Zohar consists of secrets of the Torah that Rabbi Shimon bar Yochai revealed after emerging from his thirteen years of hiding in a cave while evading the Romans. Among the souls who conveyed Torah to Rabbi Shimon are Moses, Elijah the prophet, and Adam. Scholars identify Tikunei Zohar as a text composed in the fourteenth century. The **70** chapters of Tikunei Zohar are all based on variations of readings of the first word of the Torah, בראשית (*b'reishit*).

Although there are no vowel points in the Torah, tradition teaches that there is a dagesh, a dot, in the first bet of the Torah.

> Here is the point within the palace [the dot in the bet]. The dot is a yud, associated with higher wisdom. The bet itself is the palace, Binah, understanding. Chochmah, higher wisdom, resides within the palace. The point is utterly hidden thought, closed up inside the bet (Tikun 5:2).

Sefer HaBahir
First Century CE

This book of Kabbalah first appeared in the twelfth century, but it is traditionally attributed to Rabbi Nehunia ben HaKana, one of the sages of the first century CE. The source of the title is mentioned at the very beginning of the book.

> Rabbi Nehunia ben HaKana said: One verse states, "And now they have not seen the Light, bahir bright though it be in the skies" (Job 37:21). Another verse, however, states, "He made darkness His hiding place" (Psalms 18:12). And it is also written, "Cloud and gloom surround Him" (Psalms 97:2). These two verses are in apparent contradiction to the first. Another verse comes and reconciles this apparent contradiction. It is written, "Even darkness is not dark to

You. Night shines like day, light and darkness are the same" (Psalms 139:12 and Sefer HaBahir Chapter 1, based on Aryeh Kaplan's translation).

Pirkei Avot, Ethics of the Fathers
Final edition approximately 200 CE

Pirkei Avot is a tractate of the Mishnah compiled by Rabbi Yehudah ha-Nasi. It comprises statements of the sages regarding ethical and spiritual behavior in the light of Torah.

> **Rabbi Yehoshua ben Levi said: The tablets were the work of God and the writing was the writing of God engraved in the tablets (Shmot 32:16). Don't read charut engraved, rather cherut freedom. For only a person who engages with Torah is free** (Ethics of the Fathers 6:2).

Midrash Tanchuma
Tenth Century

Midrash Tanchuma is a compilation of midrashim from different sources. Its text is estimated to have been completed more than a thousand years ago. The title refers to Rabbi Tanchuma, who lived in the third century, as some of the midrashim are reported in his name.

> **When the Holy One, blessed be He, created His world, He took counsel with Torah, as the verse says: "I have good counsel and sound wisdom. I am understanding, I have strength" (Proverbs 8:14). And Torah, with what was it written? With black fire upon white fire. As the verse says: "His locks are curls black as a raven"** (Song of Songs 5:11).

Rabbi Shlomo ben Yitzchak, Rashi
1040-1105 France

Rabbi Shlomo ben Yitzchak wrote comprehensive commentaries on almost all of the Hebrew Bible and the Babylonian Talmud. His grandsons finished these monumental projects after his death. Rashi's commentaries are the authoritative starting point for scholars. His writing is brief and direct, addressing difficult words and phrases in the text. Rashi often quotes Midrashic sources.

> These are the generations of the heavens and the earth בהבראם *(b'hibaram)* when they were created (B'reishit 2:4). Quoting the Midrash, Rashi teaches: We can read the word בהבראם *(b'hibaram)* as two words, בה בראם *(b'heh baram)*, which means with the letter heh they were created. God created the two worlds with two letters of the divine name. This world is created with the letter heh. And the world to come is created with the letter yud (B'reishit 3:2).

Rabbi Abraham ben Meir Ibn Ezra
1089-1164 Spain

Rabbi Abraham ben Meir Ibn Ezra was a Bible commentator, philosopher, astrologer, grammarian, and poet. He was a contemporary of Yehuda HaLevi, author of the Kuzari. In addition to his Bible commentary, he wrote Yesod Morah, The Foundation of Awe, his philosophy of Torah and mitzvahs, as well as various treatises on Hebrew language and grammar.

> The vastness of all existence is created and enlivened by God. He fashions all existence, and He is all existence.... The soul of man is of a higher reality than this world. It is not a physical entity, yet it fills and enlivens the body (B'reishit 1:26).

Rabbi Avraham ben David, Raavad

1125-1198 France

Rabbi Avraham ben David is best known for authoring Hasagot HaRaavad, a commentary on Rambam's Mishnah Torah. He was the father of the early Spanish Kabbalist, Isaac the Blind. Raavad is commonly identified as the author of the famous commentary on Sefer Yetzirah, but Rabbi Moshe Cordevero identifies Rabbi Yosef ben Shalom Ashkenazi as the true author.

> **The soul is composed of the holy letters that are ordered in correspondence with the mitzvahs. When a person observes the mitzvahs, he brings life and peace to his soul from upper worlds. From the limbs of the soul, life and love will come to strengthen every limb of his body** (Commentary to Sefer Yetzirah 3:2).

Rabbi Moshe ben Maimon, Rambam

1138-1204 Spain, Turkey, Egypt

Rabbi Moshe ben Maimon's (Maimonides) Mishnah Torah, a codification of the entire Talmud, is unsurpassed in its clarity of language and precision. His magnum opus in Jewish philosophy is The Guide for the Perplexed. Both of these works are an essential part of any Jewish library.

> **The Holy One recognizes His truth and knows it as it is. He does not know with a knowledge that is external to Him in the way that we know, for we and our knowledge are not one. Rather, the Creator, He, His knowledge, and His life are one from all sides and corners, in all manners of unity.... He is the Knower. He is the subject of Knowledge, and He is the Knowledge itself. All is one** (Hilchot Yesodei HaTorah 2:10).

Rabbi Moshe ben Nachman, Ramban
1194-1270 Spain, Israel

Rabbi Moshe ben Nachman (Nachmanides) is a towering figure in post-Maimonidean Jewish scholarship. He is a Halachist, Talmudic scholar, philosopher, mystic, and Bible commentator. He often took the mystical perspective on the Torah in distinction to Maimonides' rational approach.

> **The Torah preceded the creation of the world. It was written with letters of black fire on a background of white fire. Moses wrote the Torah like a scribe copying from an ancient manuscript** (Introduction to Commentary on B'reishit).

Rabbeinu Bachaya ben Asher
1255-1340 Spain, Israel

Rabbeinu Bachaya was a student of the eminent Talmudist Rabbi Shlomo ben Aderet, the Rashba. His major work is his great commentary on the Torah that often explicates a verse from four perspectives: Pshat, Midrash, Sechel, and Kabbalah.

> **"And God spoke to Moses saying." Saying means say to the people of Israel. Saying also indicates the subtle and hidden aspects of Torah. All words of Torah have both their revealed and hidden aspects. The revealed is the apparent form; the hidden is the interior, which not every reader can grasp in its subtlety** (Parshat Bo).

Rabbi Yaakov ben Asher, Baal HaTurim

1269-1343 Germany, Spain

Rabbi Yaakov, the son of Rabbi Asher, the Rosh, wrote the code of Jewish law called Arba Turim, The Four Columns, a reference to the four columns of gems on the High Priest's breastplate. The Arba Turim addresses Jewish life outside the land of Israel. His structure is adapted by Rabbi Yosef Caro in his Shulchan Aruch. Rabbi Yaakov also wrote one conventional commentary on the Torah and one collection of gematriot, hints, and acronyms.

> בראשית ברא *(B'reishit bara)* In the beginning He created has the same gematria as בראש השנה נברא העולם *(b'rosh hashanah nivrah haolam)* On Rosh Hashanah the world was created. The word בראשית *(b'reishit)* is the six first letters of בראשונה ראה אלקים שיקבלו ישראל תורה *(barishona ra'ah elokim sheyikablu Yisrael Torah)* In the beginning God saw that Israel would receive the Torah (Baal HaTurim, B'reishit).

Shulchan Aruch

Sixteenth Century

Shulchan Aruch, The Set Table, was written in the middle of the sixteenth century by Rabbi Yoseph Caro. Although preceded by Mishneh Torah and Arba Turim, Shulchan Aruch has been the major code of Jewish law since its publication. It includes additions by Rabbi Moshe Isserles that explicate the specific Halacha of the Ashkenazi world.

> One should recite Shma with fear and awe, trembling and exertion. These words that I command you today (D'varim

> 6:6).... **Every day these words should be as if they are new to you, not like one who has already heard them many times, and they are not as precious to him** (Shulchan Aruch, Orach Chayyim 61:1-2).

Rabbi Eliyahu deVidas

1518-1587 Israel

Rabbi Eliyahu deVidas was a student of Rabbi Moshe Cordevero and Rabbi Yitzchak Luria. His book Reishit Chochmah, The Beginning of Wisdom, comprises five sections: The Gates of Fear, Love, Return, Holiness, and Humility. The title and purpose of the book comes from the verse: The beginning of wisdom is the fear of God (Psalms **111**:10).

> **The vowels that determine the particular sounds of the Hebrew letters appear as little dots and dashes, but in truth they shine like the sun, an unbounded spiritual power. And so too should the letters be understood. Even the finest line crowning the letter yud is the foundation of many worlds** (Reishit Chochmah, Shaar HaYirah 4:35).

Rabbi Yehudah Loew ben Bezalel, Maharal

1520-1609 Prague

Moreinu HaRav Loew was a prolific author of many works on Jewish philosophy, Bible commentary, and Halacha, including Tiferet Yisrael, Gur Aryeh, Derech Chayim, Be'er HaGolah, and Gevurat HaShem. Maharal conveys many Kabbalistic concepts without using Kabbalistic terminology. His thought greatly influenced the Chassidic masters.

> Know, regarding the crowns and fine adornments of the Hebrew letters: Just as the letters of the Torah communicate the revealed Torah, so the crowns and fine lines indicate the very fine spiritual dimensions of Torah (Tiferet Yisrael, Chapter 63).

Rabbi Moshe Cordevero, Ramak

1522-1570 Israel

Rabbi Moshe Cordevero was a student of Rabbi Shlomo Alkabetz, who wrote Lecha Dodi. He authored many works on the Kabbalah, including the encyclopedic Pardes Rimonim, addressing all major concepts in pre-Lurianic Kabbalah; Or Yakar, a comprehensive commentary on the Zohar; and Tomer Devorah, a guide to becoming "In the Image of God" through the path of the sefirot.

> The Hebrew letters are totally spiritual in their essence. The shapes of our letters correspond to twenty-two states of spiritual essence (Pardes Rimonim 27:2).

Rabbi Mordechai Yaffe, Baal HaLevushim

1530-1612 Prague

Rabbi Mordechai Yaffe was a contemporary of the Maharal. He wrote his own version of the Shulchan Aruch, Levush Malchut, as well as commentaries on both *The Guide for the Perplexed* and Sefer Recanati. His Halachic work includes a brief description of each letter's shape and Kabbalistic connotations.

> Our predecessors were masters; they knew the Halachic reasoning and significance of every detail of the law. And they wrote in a terse, abbreviated style. Their manner is like excellent but unsalted food. We need the addition of the salt to bring out the taste. For what is a law without a taste of its significance? (Preface to the Levush Techelet in Levush Malchut)

Rabbi Yitzchak Luria Ashkenazi, Ari or Arizal

1534-1572 Egypt, Israel

Adoneinu (Our Master) Rabbi Yitzchak was born in Jerusalem but grew up in Cairo. He was educated in traditional Talmudic study and then became a devoted student of the Zohar. He is reported to have spent seven years in meditative seclusion by the Nile River. At age 25 he returned to Israel and made his way to Safed. He was briefly a student of Rabbi Moshe Cordevero. All of Luria's teachings are from manuscripts written, collected, and edited by his devoted students Rabbi Chayim Vital and his son Rabbi Shmuel Vital. These voluminous writings were only from the last two years of Luria's life.

> When the Divine Will wanted to create in order to benefit His creations so that they would recognize His greatness, and merit to be a chariot above, and cling to Him, He emanated a single point comprising the ten imperceptible sefirot (Etz Chayim, Shaar HaClalim, Chapter 1).
>
> The twenty-two letters are the 248 limbs of the body. The five final letters, מנצפ״ך (*mem, nun, tzadi, peh, kaf*), are the blood. The tagim (fine lines on the letters) are the nefesh that rests on the blood. The essential place where the nefesh rests is

the heart. The vowels are the ruach. The cantillation notes are the neshama. And the thirty-two paths of wisdom are the entire body and soul (Etz Chayim, Shaar Tanta, Chapter 6).

Rabbi Isaiah Horowitz, Shlah

1555-1630 Prague, Israel

Rabbi Isaiah Horowitz is best known for his work Shnei Luchos HaBris (Shlah), Two Tablets of the Covenant. The book provides a fascinating mystical perspective on Torah, quoting liberally from Zohar, Rabbi Moshe Cordevero, Rabbi Meir ibn Gabbai, and Rabbi Yitzchak Luria.

> **People think that the realm of the sod hidden is something separate from the revealed, but it is not so! As the nature of the hidden becomes dense and ultimately physical — that is the revealed!** (Shlah, Introduction to Toldot Adam)

Rabbi Israel ben Eliezer, Besht

1698-1760 Ukraine

The Baal Shem Tov's life and teaching is the foundation of Chassidic Judaism. He wrote no books, but his students refer to his teachings frequently. Two prominent collections of his teachings are Baal Shem Tov on the Torah and Keter Shem Tov.

> **The letter aleph is identified with the aluph, the ultimate and hidden source and authority of all creation. All the other letters are generated from the aleph. Bet, the second letter, is like two alephs. Gimel, three alephs. Tav, the last letter, is like 400 alephs. Aleph is the source of all letters of Torah. It is closest to the infinite and unformed light, the Eyn Sof.**

> After aleph, each letter is a thicker garment enclosing the light of the previous letter (Toldot Yaakov Yosef, VaYetze).

Rabbi Dov Ber, Maggid of Mezritch
1704-1772 Poland

Rabbi Dov Ber, the great student of the Baal Shem Tov, ultimately succeeded his teacher in leading and developing the Chassidic movement in Eastern Europe. Among his many students are the pillars of the Chassidic world: Rabbi Shneur Zalman (Chabad), Rabbi Levi Yitzchak of Berditchev, Rabbi Elimelech of Lizensk, and Rabbi Menachem Nachum of Chernobyl.

> **Each letter of each word of prayer is a great and limitless spiritual world. Each letter pronounced awakens its corresponding spiritual essence. Therefore, recite your prayer with great energy and overwhelming joy** (Klalim Noraim Vehanhagot, Torat HaMaggid).

Rabbi Moshe Chayim Luzzato, Ramchal
1707-1746 Italy, Holland, Israel

Rabbi Moshe Chayim Luzzato was an Italian Kabbalist and poet. His genius brought him into constant conflict with the Italian rabbinic authorities. In Holland he composed many of his best-known works, before moving to Israel. His books include *The Way of God* and *The Path of the Just.*

> **This Torah that is present before us, all its words and letters are like a burning coal. A casual glance will see a low burning**

coal. But a person who engages with the Torah will see a flame rise from every letter, full of colors and hues. These are the levels of understanding concealed in each and every letter (Derech Etz Chayim).

Rabbi Yaakov Yosef of Polnoye

1710-1784 Ukraine

Rabbi Yaakov Yosef was a foremost disciple of the Baal Shem Tov. Toldot Yaakov Yosef, his book of Chassidut, quotes extensively from the teachings of his master. It is considered the first Chassidic book.

> Our vision of the perfection of the future is this: We will see in the letters of the Torah that we are learning and in the letters of the words of our prayers, that they are in truth spiritual realities of the highest realms (B'reishit).

Rabbi Menachem Nachum of Chernobyl, Meor Einayim

1730-1787 Ukraine

Rabbi Menachem Nachum was a young student of the Baal Shem Tov and disciple of Rabbi Dov Ber of Mezritch. His book, Meor Einayim, is a collection of Torah thoughts recorded and edited by his students. Family tradition reports that when his students brought him the book shortly before his death, he leafed through it and commented, "Yes. I meant that also...."

> "In the beginning God created..." meaning, with Torah God created. The energy of Torah is in everything and in all worlds. Further, Torah and God are one. We find that God's life energy is in everything and in every world (Meor Einayim, B'reishit).

Rabbi Yaakov Koppel Hager

1730-1787 Ukraine

Rabbi Yaakov Koppel Hager was a Kabbalist in the generation of the Baal Shem Tov. His writings are distinctly Kabbalistic and not Chassidic in nature. His best-known works are Shaarei Gan Eden, Gates of the Garden of Eden, and Kol Yaakov, Voice of Jacob, a commentary on the prayer book. The leaders of Kossov-Viznitz Chassidut trace their ancestry back to him.

> **My beloved brothers and friends — know that our great and inspired teacher, Rabbi Shimon Bar Yochai, prefaced his teachings with the warning: "Cursed is the man who makes a sculpted or molten image"** (D'varim 27:15). **This is to caution us that we must not imagine that we are perceiving God's light itself. Rather we must know that our perceptions, at best, are an apprehension of the vessels that carry God's light within them** (Shaarei Gan Eden, Orach Tzadikim).

Rabbi Avraham Friedman, HaMalach

1739-1776 Ukraine

Rabbi Avraham Friedman was the son of Rabbi Dov Ber of Mezritch. He is known as The Angel due to his extreme piety. His book of collected words of Torah, Chesed L'Avraham, is heavily Kabbalistic in nature. It includes comments on the Torah portion of the week as well as a short essay, Explication of the Ten Sefirot. His grandson Yisrael of Rizhyn, founded the Rizhyner dynasty that still exists today.

> Man's soul comprises the seven lower sefirot. He can use them either to glorify God's name or his own. When he uses them toward the divine, he magnifies the divine and raises himself into holiness. Each of these seven are themselves composed of seven. When these forty-nine aspects are turned toward the holy, then the fiftieth Gateway of Holiness, the Gate of Understanding, rests upon that soul. This is the **world of genuine freedom** (Introduction to Chesed L'Avraham).

Rabbi Levi Yitzchak of Berditchev

1740-1809 Ukraine

Rabbi Levi Yitzchak was a student of Rabbi Dov Ber of Mezritch and a contemporary of Rabbi Shneur Zalman, the first rebbe of Chabad. His writings on the Torah are collected in the volume Kedushat Levi, The Holiness of Levi, a reference to the elevated status of the tribe of Levi in the Torah.

> A powerful tool for spiritual attainment is to learn from the text of a sefer Torah; the letters make one wise. The letters derive from the highest point of creation, and the text of a sefer Torah is a reflection of the upper worlds (Kedusha Rishona).

Rabbi Shneur Zalman of Liadi, Baal HaTanya

1745-1812 Belarus

Rabbi Shneur Zalman is the founder of Chabad Chassidut. A towering figure in the world of Chassidic thought, he composed Sefer HaTanya, a systematic approach to divine service. Sefer

HaTanya is the foundational work of Chabad Chassidut and universally recognized in the Chassidic world as a necessary classic. He authored an important Halachic work, Shulchan Aruch HaRav, as well as teachings on the weekly Torah portion, Torah Or and Likutei Torah. He also wrote commentaries on the prayer book, Siddur HaRav.

> Every act of divine creation is called a ma'amar, a divine utterance, a sequence of letters. The letters of יהי אור *(yehi or)* let there be light, are God's ways of transmitting His chesed love into the light of creation (Tanya, The Gate of Unity and Faith, Chapter 11).

Rabbi Moshe Chayim Efraim, Degel Machane Efraim

1748-1800 Ukraine

Rabbi Moshe Chayim Efraim was a grandson of the Baal Shem Tov and brother of Rabbi Baruch of Mezebiz. He grew up in the presence of the Baal Shem Tov and later studied under the Maggid of Mezritch and Rabbi Yaakov Yosef of Polnoye.

> The purpose of our lives is to raise Shechina up out of the dust of the world. When a Jew takes this as his goal and intends all of his actions to illuminate and raise up Shechina, the Shechina will also raise him up from his fallen state (B'reishit).

Rabbi Mordechai Twersky

1770-1837 Ukraine

Rabbi Mordechai Twersky was the son of the Meor Einayim. He was the second rabbi of Chernobyl and is known as the Chernobler Maggid. His eight sons all became rebbes in the Chassidic world, including the communities of Skver, Rachmastrivka, and Tolna. Rabbi Mordechai's book of Torah teachings is simply named Likutei Torah, A Collection of Torah. Many books bear that generic title.

> **When you speak, speak with all of your 248 limbs and 365 sinews…. Come with all your powers into your speech. Then your speech will be a whole vessel. But first you must break the previous vessel, and realize that what you have accomplished to date is not the wholeness you must seek now** (Likutei Torah, page 59).

Rabbi Yitzchak Meir Rothenberg Alter, Chidushei HaRim

1799-1866 Poland

Rabbi Yitzchak Meir was the first rebbe of Ger Chassidut, the grandfather of the Sfat Emet. He was a student of the Kotzker Rebbe. His writings are Talmudic commentaries and Chassidic thought, all under the title Chidushei HaRim, The Words of Torah of Rabbi Yitzchak Meir.

> **Spiritual renewal is divine light that will not become old. The world of nature ages and falls into set patterns, but Israel is connected above nature, where there is endless renewal** (Parshat Bo).

Rabbi Mordechai Yosef Leiner, Mei HaShiloach

1801-1854 Poland

Rabbi Mordechai Yosef is one of the most distinctive thinkers in Polish Chassidut of the nineteenth century. His voice continues to fascinate the modern reader. He was a student of the Kotzker Rebbe. Mei Shiloach is a collection of his observations on the Torah and Talmud, written mostly by his grandson, Rabbi Gershon Hanoch Henech of Radzin.

> **The fourth blessing in the Musaf Amidah prayer (Tikanta Shabbat) for Sabbath is written with a series of words in reversed alphabetical order, from tav to shin, through all the letters, to bet to aleph. This teaches us that on the Sabbath all the letters are standing and facing the Creator. To man's perspective the letters are in reverse order, but on the Sabbath one must learn to see exclusively from the divine perspective** (Mei Shiloach, Likutim, Volume 2).

Rabbi Yaakov Leiner, Beit Yaakov

1828-1878 Poland

Rabbi Yaakov Leiner was the second rebbe of Ishbitza-Radzin and the son of Rabbi Mordechai Yosef, the Mei Shiloach. Many of his writings are lost — among them a commentary on the siddur and the Zohar. We have extant today three volumes of commentary on the first three books of the Torah, a book of teachings on the holidays, and a Haggadah for Passover.

> **Midrash Tanchuma states: Hear, O Israel, the Lord our God, the Lord is** אחד *(echad)* **One. If the scribe writes a** ר *(resh)*

instead of a ד (*dalet*) (by rounding the corner of the letter), it is like destroying the world. He turns (*echad*), one, into acher, another.

The Zohar says the dalet is like the squared corner of the altar. That corner is the place of recognizing and accepting the yoke of heaven. Why? The squared corner is the shape of a dalet, where two perpendicular lines meet. Man's task is not to smooth over the contradictions of life. When he confronts radical change in the direction of his life, he must understand and accept that this is from God, and he must adjust his life in adaptation of a new manifestation of the divine will (Beit Yaakov B'reishit, bet).

Rabbi Yehudah Aryeh Leib Alter, Sfat Emet

1847-1905 Poland

Rabbi Yehudah Aryeh Leib was the third rebbe of Ger Chassidut. Starting at age 23, he led the community for 35 years. He recorded in a concise and often poetic form the lessons that he delivered on Shabbat and holidays. His writings often serve as an entryway into further study of Chassidut. He is referred to by the title of his writings, Sfat Emet, The Language of Truth.

> Everything is created with the twenty-two letters of the Torah. There is nothing that does not have the spiritual form of the letters at its essence. All of creation is the garment of the Holy Letters (Bo תרל"ו ד"ה בא).

Rabbi Abraham Mordechai Alter, Imrei Emet

1865-1948 Poland, Israel

Rabbi Abraham Mordechai was the fourth rebbe of Ger. His writing on the weekly portion and the holidays is called Imrei Emet, Sayings of Truth, taking its title from his father's writing, Sfat Emet, The Language of Truth.

> Each person's soul is unique. Each one is created for a distinct divine purpose. And, as the Mishna says, each one should say "The world was created for me" (B'reishit).

Rabbi Avraham Yitzchak HaCohen Kook

1865-1935 Latvia, Israel

Rav Kook was the first Ashkenazi chief rabbi of Palestine during the British Mandate from 1921 to 1935. He is one of the most creative thinkers of the twentieth century. His prolific writings are studied with reverence by many. One short meditation he wrote on the Hebrew letters, Reish Millin, is full of Kabbalistic illusions. Among his major works are Orot, Orot HaKodesh, and Orot HaTshuvah.

> There are thoughts that precede their expression in letters. These thoughts are constantly active within us. They are shapeless forms, higher than anything familiar. We strive always to come to an awareness of these thoughts: They are the awesome beauty of the soul. We come to know their beauty as it manifests in us as the Hebrew letters. When we

begin to grasp the letters, we encounter the illumination of their vowels, song, and adornments. Then the words, phrases, verses, and entire texts radiate their splendor upon us** (Reish Millin, Introduction).

Golda Meir

1898-1978 Russia, United States, Israel

Golda Meir was the fourth prime minister of Israel, from 1969 to 1974. She was the first woman to become the head of the government in Israel. She immigrated to Israel from Wisconsin in 1921.

Rabbi Abraham Joshua Heschel

1907-1972 Poland, United States

Rabbi Abraham Joshua Heschel was one of the greatest and most influential Jewish thinkers of the twentieth century. He was born into a Polish Chassidic family and earned an Orthodox rabbinic ordination before pursuing a doctorate at the University of Berlin. His many books include *God in Search of Man*, *The Prophets*, *The Sabbath*, and *A Passion for Truth*.

> "Hasidism was neither a sect nor a doctrine. It was a dynamic approach to reality.... In attaching oneself to the source of all unity, the Hasid learned to bend every action to the ultimate goal.... The Hasid studied the Talmud also to experience its soul, to envision worlds" (*The Circle of the Baal Shem Tov: Studies in Hasidism*, Introduction).

Rabbi Aryeh Kaplan
1934-1983 United States

Rabbi Aryeh Kaplan was a prolific writer and translator of classical Jewish texts including Kabbalistic works such as Sefer Yetzirah and Sefer HaBahir. He also translated and wrote a commentary on the Torah, *The Living Torah*. He wrote introductions to Jewish spirituality including *Meditation and Kabbalah* and *Inner Space*. Rabbi Kaplan died suddenly at the age of 49. In the last decade of his life, he wrote more than twenty-five books.

> "The idea of Kabbalah... is to become completely infused with Torah and to connect with it on every possible level. Without Kabbalah, a person could understand Torah on a number of levels. The only way to grasp every single nuance of Torah... is through the prophetic wisdom that is contained in Kabbalah" (*Inner Space*, Chapter 1).

Rabbi Adin Steinsaltz
1937-2020 Israel

Rabbi Adin Steinsaltz was a prolific writer and scholar who changed the landscape of Talmud study with his editions of Talmud, making it accessible to a wide audience with his clear running commentary. His motto was "Let my people know." Among his many publications are *The Thirteen Petalled Rose*, *The Essential Talmud*, and his edition of Maimonides' Mishnah Torah. He also wrote extensively on Chabad philosophy.

> "No thought can grasp You at all" (Tikunei Zohar). That statement is meant to be understood literally. There is no level of thought, even that which is radically superior and

more sophisticated than human thought [such as angelic thought], that can grasp the Holy One. It is not at all within the grasp of any Higher Thought. The nature of the Holy One is truly Eyn Sofit, limitless, beyond any boundary or definition (*The Thirteen Petalled Rose*, Hebrew edition, Chapter 13).

Matok MiDvash
2003-2004 Israel

Matok MiDvash is the title of a contemporary translation of the entire Aramaic text of the Zohar into Hebrew, and a commentary written by Rabbi Daniel Frisch, based on the classical Zohar commentators such as Rabbi Moshe Cordevero, Rabbi Yitzchak Luria, and Rabbi Moshe Zacuto.

> "God looked into the Torah and created the world." This means that God looked at the twenty-two letters of the Torah and the ten utterances of creation. These are the essence of the thirty-two pathways of wisdom. They correspond to the thirty-two times God's name, Elohim, appears in the creation story (Zohar 2:161b).

Nurit G'al Dor
Twenty-first Century Israel

Nurit G'al Dor is a student of Rabbi Moshe Bleicher of Yeshivat Shavei Chevron. Rabbi Bleicher was a student of Rabbi Tzvi Yehudah Kook. Nurit writes books of commentary on the Tanach with a passionate intention to increase the reader's faith in God and the purpose of the Jewish people. She teaches women in seminaries in Israel.

> The Torah teaches us the way to meet The Soul of the world, with the inner essence of its vitality, and to bring it forth from potential into actuality (Zera Avraham Ohavi).

Rabbi Shlomo Rosenberg

Twenty-first Century Israel

Rabbi Shlomo Rosenberg is a graduate of Har Etzion Yeshiva in Israel. He teaches Gemara and Jewish thought. He is the author of Tikun L'ad, Teachings of the Sfat Emet.

> Holiness is the foundation of all creation. By looking deeply into even ordinary reality we can learn to recognize God's word speaking to us. (Tikun L'ad, page 15)

Bibliography

- Alter, Michael J. *Why the Torah Begins with the Letter Beit* (New Jersey: Jason Aronson Inc., 1998).

- Estes, Clarissa Pinkola, Ph.D. *Women Who Run With the Wolves: Myths and Stories of the Wild Woman Archetype* (New York: Ballantine Books, 1992).

- G'al Dor, Nurit. Zerah Avraham Ohavi (Jerusalem: Shalmei Ariel, 2002).

- Heschel, Abraham Joshua. *Man Is Not Alone: A Philosophy of Religion* (New York: Farrar, Straus and Giroux, 1976).

- Heschel, Abraham J. Edited by Samuel H. Dresner. *The Circle of the Baal Shem Tov: Studies in Hasidism* (Chicago: University of Chicago Press, 1985).

- *JPS Hebrew-English Tanakh* תנ"ך (Philadelphia: The Jewish Publication Society, 1999).

- Kamenetz, Rodger. *The Jew in the Lotus: A Poet's Rediscovery of Jewish Identity in Buddhist India* (New York: Harper Collins, 1995).

- Kaplan, Aryeh. *Sefer Yetzirah: The Book of Creation In Theory and Practice*, Revised Edition (New York: Weiser Books, 1997).

- Kaplan, Rabbi Aryeh. *Inner Space: Introduction to Kabbalah, Meditation and Prophecy* (New York: Moznaim, 1990).

- Kook, Abraham Isaac HaCohen. Chadarav/Collection of Personal Writings (Israel: Reut, 2001).

- Kook, Abraham Isaac HaCohen. Orot HaKodesh, Vol. 3 (Jerusalem: The Rav Kook Institute, 1963).

- Kook, Abraham Isaac HaCohen. Reish Millin (Jerusalem: HaMosad HaRav Kook, 1994).

- Kook, Abraham Isaac HaCohen. Ain Ayah (Jerusalem: Rav Tzvi Yehudah HaCohen Kook, 1994).

- Kook, Abraham Isaac HaCohen. Maamarei HaRaAyah (Jerusalem: Golda Ketz [zal] Foundation, 1983).

- Kook, Abraham Isaac HaCohen. Olot HaRaAyah (Jerusalem: Mosad HaRav Kook, 1985).

- Rosenberg, Shlomo. Tikon L'Ad (Alon Shvut: Yeshiva Har Tzion, 2007).

- Rowling, J.K. *Harry Potter and the Sorcerer's Stone* (New York: Scholastic Press, 1998).

- Steinsaltz, Rabbi Adin. *The Thirteen Petalled Rose: A Discourse on the Essence of Jewish Existence and Belief* (New Jersey: Jason Aronson Inc., 1980).

- Steinsaltz, Rabbi Adin. Shlosha Asar Alei HaShoshana, Hebrew edition (Jerusalem: Maggid, 2010).

- Tatz, Akiva, and Gottlieb, David. *Letters to a Buddhist Jew* (New York: Targum/Feldheim, 2004).

- Tenen, Stan. *The Alphabet That Changed the World: How Genesis Preserves a Science of Consciousness in Geometry and Gesture* (California: North Atlantic Books, 2011).

- Tolkien, J.R.R. *The Lord of the Rings* (Glasgow: Harper Collins, 1995).

- Baal Shem Tov, Israel Ben Eliezer (Jerusalem: Machon Daat Yosef, 1991).

- Be'er haGolah, Yehudah Loew (Jerusalem: Yahadut, 1971).

- Beit Yaakov, Yaakov Leiner (Jerusalem: Rabbi J. Lainer Publisher, 2009).

- Chesed L'Avraham, Avraham Friedman HaMalach (Jerusalem: Siftei Tzadikim, 1995).

- Degel Machane Efraim, Moshe Chayim Efraim of Sudlikov (Jerusalem: Mir, 1994).

- Derech Etz Chayim, Moshe Chaim Luzzato (Jerusalem: Eshkol, 1978).

- Derech HaShem, Moshe Chayim Luzatto (Jerusalem: Feldheim, 1983).

- Etz Chayim, Yitzchak Luria (Jerusalem: Mekor Chayim, 1963).

- Hilchot Yesodei haTorah, Moshe ben Maimon, Maimonides (Jerusalem: Koren, 2020).

- Imrei Emet, Avraham Mordechai (Tel Aviv: Binyamin Menachem Alter).

- Kedushat Levi, Levi Yitzchak of Berdichev (Israel: Machon Kedushat Levi, 2007).

- Klalim Noraim v'Hanhagot, Dov Ber of Mezritch (Bnei Berak: Peer haSefer, 1976).

- Levush Malchut, Mordechai Yafe (Bnei Berak: Mesorah, 1983).

- Likutei Torah, Mordechai Twersky of Chernobyl (Israel: Even Israel, 1986).

- Maggid D'varav L'Yaakov, Dov Ber of Mezritch (New York: Kehot, 1979).

- Mei HaShiloach, Mordechai Yosef Leiner (Bnei Berak: Mishor, 1995).

- Meor Einayim, Menachem Nachum (Bnei Berak: Nachalat Tzvi, 2015).

- Midrash Rabbah (Tel Aviv: Yavneh, 1981).

- Mishneh Torah, Moshe ben Maimon, Maimonides (Jerusalem: Moznaim, 1990).

- Netivot Olam, Yehudah Loew (Tel Aviv: Yad Mordechai, 1997).

- Or Torah, Dov Ber of Mezritch (New York: Kehot, 1980).

- Pardes Rimonim, Moshe Cordevero (Jerusalem: Yerid HaSefarim, 2000).

- Rabbeinu Bachaye al HaTorah (Jerusalem: Mosad HaRav Kook, 1981).

- Ramban Commentary, Moshe ben Nachman, Nachmanides (Jerusalem: Mosad HaRav Kook, 1960).

- Reishit Chochmah, Rabbi Eliyahu deVidas (Jerusalem: Torah MeTzion, 2000).

- Sefer haBahir, Commentary by Aryeh Kaplan (York Beach, Maine: Samuel Weiser, 1979).

- Sefer Yetzirah (Jerusalem: Yeshivat HaChayim Vehashalom, 1990).

- Sfat Emet, Rabbi Yehudah Aryeh Lev Alter of Ger (Israel: HaMachon HaTorani Yeshivat Or Etzion, 2000).

- Shaarei Gan Eden, Rabbi Yaakov Koppel (Jerusalem: Yerid HaSefarim, 2005).

- Shnei Luchot HaBrit, Rabbi Isaiah Horowitz (Jerusalem: Oz Vehadar, 1993).

- Tanya, Rabbi Schneur Zalman (New York: Kehot, 1980).
- Tiferet Yisrael, Rabbi Yehudah Loew (Tel Aviv: Machon Yad Mordechai, 1979).
- Toldot Yaakov Yosef, Rabbi Yaakov Yosef from Polnoy (Bnei Berak: Nachalat Tzvi, 2016).
- Zohar, Matok MiDvash, commentary by Rabbi Daniel Frisch (Jerusalem: Machon Daat Yosef, 2003-2004).

www.ingramcontent.com/pod-product-compliance
Lightning Source LLC
Chambersburg PA
CBHW032139160426
43197CB00008B/704